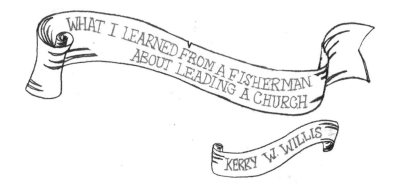

RELATIONAL LEADERSHIP

WHAT I LEARNED FROM A FISHERMAN ABOUT LEADING A CHURCH

KERRY W. WILLIS

BEACON HILL PRESS
OF KANSAS CITY

Printed in the
United States of America

Cover Design: J.R. Caines
Internal Design: Sharon Page

Library of Congress Cataloging-in-Publication Data

Willis, Kerry W., 1961-
  Relational leadership : what I learned from a fisherman about leading
a church / Kerry W. Willis.
    p. cm.
  Includes bibliographical references (p.   ).
  ISBN 978-0-8341-2472-1 (pbk.)
  1. Christian leadership. I. Title.
  BV652.1.W513 2009
  253—dc22

                                                          2009024955

10 9 8 7 6 5 4 3 2 1

CONTENTS

FOREWORD

There are those who preach sermons, and there are those who live a message. Kerry Willis is the latter. He desires, as I do, to be known for his walk not his work. This book is not just for pastors but for all who desire to live out Jesus' prayer that we would be *one*.

Relational Leadership will help you understand that getting along is not about seeing things alike but about the higher call to live in love. It is written in a style that makes it an easy read. It is the kind of book I wish I could have read early in my ministry. *Relational Leadership* is about focusing on what is most important and about not getting lost in the drive for success. In this book you will find practical truth, and hopefully it will help some leaders find their way back to the joy of ministry.

I think *Relational Leadership* answers the question, "If I did everything God wanted me to do, would I be doing more or less?" I am convinced for many it would be *less*. Kerry's lifestyle of ministry is proof that a person does not have to burn out to be an effective leader, especially an effective relational leader.

—James Spruill
Evangelist, Church of the Nazarene

I AM SO GRATEFUL

This book may be really more a journey of simplicity than a journal of specifics, more about living and giving than writing and citing. But whatever this book is, I do want to dedicate it to my tender mom, my fisherman dad, and my generous granny (she's with Jesus now). Without my mom's prayers, my dad's words, and my granny's love, I really would not have much to share that would be worth having, or anywhere to lead that would be worth going. Without a doubt, this devoted trio, Mom, Dad, and Granny, teamed up with the One called Wonderful, Jesus, to teach me and to reach me personally with the reality that relationships rule! They didn't teach me this No. 1 life lesson by finger-pointing or wordy preaching, quite the contrary. Mostly, they just taught me this truth by their God-ordered practices, Jesus-led patterns, and Spirit-filled passions.

My God has a name. He is *Faithful.* My family has a name. They are *Precious.* I have a name. I am *Grateful.* I would like to pray now: "Abba Father, Daddy God, I'm so grateful to You for my dear mom, Lady Melba, and for my devoted dad,

Captain Billy, and for the memory of my delightful Granny Margery. I'm most especially grateful for Your Darling of Heaven, who is my heart's desire, Jesus. I am so grateful to be the son of a fisherman and a fisherman for the Son. Because I hunger and thirst for a right relationship with You, I'm blessed. Nothing I desire compares with You. Amen"

As I begin this project it is a sacred day. "Happy Anniversary, Kim Annette. Beyond many years I will love you, yes, always and forever. Thanks for being my Simon of Cyrene. Yes, thanks for helping me carry the ministry cross. It's our glorious burden to follow nail-pierced footprints—more glorious than burden. Thanks for loving Jesus. Thanks for loving me. Thanks for loving our nearly grown children, Grayson Kent and Allison Brette, and for caring for our Jack Russell beagle, Oreo Pup. Indeed, as a married couple we know relationships rule—beyond many years, yes, always and forever."

Grateful,

Kerry

WELCOME TO THE JOURNEY

Jesus taught fishermen relational leadership, and He has surely used fishermen to teach me relational leadership—especially one fisherman, who I call "Daddy."

Yes, my fisherman dad taught me that everything really rises and falls on *relationships*. Yes, even *leadership*. Especially *leadership*. If we want to really lead in the local church and beyond, we must embrace wholeheartedly one undeniable reality—*relationships rule!* We must also know the *rules of relationships;* that is, we must know and more importantly model and communicate realistic leadership expectations to those who partner alongside us in leading others.

So, welcome to the journey. Up ahead we'll discover some simple but profound rules of relationships. It's a baker's dozen, yes, thirteen realistic expectations for those who desire to lead in the local church and beyond. Many of these insights I learned from my father, a shrimp boat captain who taught me more about relational leadership than anyone I know.

My dad was always a model of servant leadership to me. His crew members throughout the years knew that to work alongside Captain Billy was just that—a real relationship alongside a captain who compassionately cared for them and clearly communicated realistic expectations. Whenever I invite others to join our leadership team, to come alongside me, my dad's expectations are central to the thirteen I communicate clearly to these prospective team members. These expectations are, in my opinion, the nonnegotiable rules of servant leadership, especially for those of us who envision Jesus living within us to be a relational reality and not a religious requirement.

Now, exhale, smile, and relax, and together, with ears wide open, let's hear the voice of our Lord inside of us. Jesus has already been this way before, and now He wants to lead us on a journey that overflows with the joy of realistic leadership expectations. If we will go, the One called Wonderful will whisper the promise of His presence to us: "Surely I am with you always" (Matt. 28:20). As our journey together begins, I envision His banner waving just ahead: Relationships Rule!

REALISTIC EXPECTATION №.13
BE GENEROUS AND GRATEFUL

Like the Top 10 Countdown on *Late Show with David Letterman,* our baker's dozen starts with the last biscuit placed in the basket and finishes with the first. So we begin our countdown with Realistic Expectation No. 13.

At sunset one evening in Colorado Springs, I was traveling west toward Pikes Peak when my heart leaped within me. Remembering God's love in my life, I just cried out in worship: "Your name is Faithful. My name is Grateful!" Ever since that moment, almost always when I sign my name, I include the word "grateful." In light of God's love, if we as His followers are to be known by two descriptive titles, surely *generous* and *grateful* are appropriate. Don't you agree?

BEFORE GOD AS AN OFFERING

In *The Message* paraphrase of the Holy Bible, Rom. 12:1 lays out beautifully the realistic expectation of being generous and grateful. Here it is: "So here's what I want you to do, God helping you: Take your everyday, ordinary life—your sleeping, eating, going-to-work, and walking-around life—and place it before God as an offering."

Religion often calls for dead martyrs, but relationships call for living sacrifices. If we choose to allow the Holy Spirit to have His way in our lives, generosity and gratitude will characterize the way we live. If we refuse to allow the Holy Spirit to have His way in our lives, stinginess and dissatisfaction will characterize the way we die.

I want to be an offering for God, not an offense to God. Those who lead alongside me must have the same desires. When God places His thumb on my life, I want to be like a grape, not a marble. When pressed, a marble resists and shoots off in its own direction, but a grape gives all it has to the one doing the pressing.

I'm so glad Jesus was a generous and grateful Son of God and Son of Man. I am also glad He chose to be a grape and not a marble when He came to Gethsemane, the place of pressing. He prayed the perfect prayer to the Father: "Not my will, but thine, be done" (Luke 22:42, KJV). I'm so glad Jesus obeyed the will of His parents—God of heaven and Mary of Nazareth. At Cana of Galilee, Jesus obeyed His earthly mother's will and made wine for the wedding guests. In Gethsemane, Jesus obeyed His Heavenly Father's will and became wine for the whole world. Why did He do it? He was generous and grateful. He proved that *relationships rule* by placing His life before His Father God as an offering.

REMEMBERING PASSION WEEK

During a recent pilgrimage to Jerusalem, my prayer partner, Steve Thigpen, and I chose a Thursday night to share Holy Communion together. We then left our guesthouse within the Old City walls, exited the Zion Gate near the traditional location of the Last Supper, and walked outside the city gate along the Kidron Valley all the way up to Gethsemane on the Mount of Olives. Whatever you can imagine, it was that wonderful and invigorating and humbling and more. Walking where Jesus walked as Jesus walks within you is an indescribable experience of intimacy for a fully devoted follower of Jesus.

Did Jesus ever prove His generosity and gratitude any more than He did on that Thursday night before His crucifixion? Think about it. The Son of God washing the feet of fishermen? Does it get any more generous than that? Then, once He was in the olive grove, out of love and gratitude for His Father, Jesus surrendered His own life's blood so we could be in relationship with heaven again. *Wow* is right! When the mad mob came to Gethsemane, Jesus could have easily slipped out the back entrance and escaped to Bethany, but He did not do it. Instead our Lord turned himself over to the bloodthirsty bunch and said, "Let my followers go" (John 18:8, author's paraphrase). Surely Jesus modeled and clearly communicated to His disciples and to us on that night a realistic leadership expectation, the relationship rule that calls us to be generous and grateful. If we want to lead as Jesus led, we will be grateful to God and generous to God and to one another.

As I study the Holy Scriptures surrounding the Passion Week of our Lord, I'm convinced that one woman's very personal and quite public response of generosity and gratitude may have helped Jesus to stay on the Cross. The story unfolds in the first few verses of Mark 14. *The Message* paraphrase records it this way:

> Jesus was at Bethany, a guest of Simon the Leper. While he was eating dinner, a woman came up carrying a bottle of very expensive perfume. Opening the bottle, she poured it on his head. Some of the guests became furious among themselves. "That's criminal! A sheer waste! This perfume could have been

sold for well over a year's wages and handed out to the poor." They swelled up in anger, nearly bursting with indignation over her.

But Jesus said, "Let her alone. Why are you giving her a hard time? She has just done something wonderfully significant for me. You will have the poor with you every day for the rest of your lives. Whenever you feel like it, you can do something for them. Not so with me. She did what she could when she could— she pre-anointed my body for burial. And you can be sure that wherever in the whole world the Message is preached, what she just did is going to be talked about admiringly."

Judas Iscariot, one of the Twelve, went to the cabal of high priests, determined to betray him. They couldn't believe their ears, and promised to pay him well. He started looking for just the right moment to hand him over. (Vv. 3-11)

This is a very powerful passage. It ends with the selfish attitude of one greedy male disciple, but it begins with the selfless act of worship of one generous female convert. Let's focus on her selfless act of worship for now. The way I understand it, expensive perfume is very concentrated and intended to be used the way the old hair formula slogan of the 1960s recommended: "A little dab'll do ya." But *no,* this woman had generosity and gratitude that had to be expressed extravagantly. She dumped the whole bottle on the head of her Lord. I'd say Jesus got the opposite effect of being sprayed by a skunk. I have no doubt that while Jesus was on the Cross, every time our Savior inhaled He could smell the sweet scent of the generous and grateful worship given to Him by the woman at Simon the Leper's house earlier in the week. Surely every time Jesus was tempted to call ten thousand angels to save himself and forget us, He must have remembered the woman worshipper who gave Him her all. How could He do any less than to give His all for her and for us?

Never underestimate the impact of being generous and grateful before the Lord and others. It has the power of very expensive, concentrated perfume being poured out all at once. In other words, when we are generous and grateful, it is simply unforgettable to God and people.

A RELIGIOUS TALK VERSUS OUR RELATIONSHIP WALK

A few years ago Greg Kellam hired our high school son, Grayson, to clean up around his motorcycle showroom. I recall the day Grayson came home with his first paycheck. His grin was contagious. I followed him to his room to talk about God-centered generosity and gratitude—tithing. To *tithe* is to return to God 10 percent of what He has given to us. If the tithe belongs to the Lord, is it really wrong to say that the remaining 90 percent belongs to us? No, it's not. Well, before I could get my 10 percent tithe talk started, our son stopped me with these words: "Dad, before you say anything, I've been thinking about my offering for Sunday. I've decided that I want to give 20 percent of my paycheck back to the Lord?" Obviously, a religious talk was not necessary. Our son had been closely watching the relationship walk of his parents. We are still humbled and believe God is still honored by the spontaneous continuation of devotion that flows from our son's tender heart. If returning to God His 10 percent proves we are grateful, could it be that gladly dipping into our remaining 90 percent proves we are generous?

Being generous and grateful are realistic expectations taught to us by Jesus. They are also two powerful relationship rules to live by and to lead from. Being generous and grateful is one unforgettable way to live the love of God out loud and to prove without doubt to a seemingly hopeless world that indeed, relationships rule!

REALISTIC EXPECTATION No. 12
BE OUTGOING AND OVERFLOWING

A summons to lead is first and foremost a call
to honor God and to help people honor God too.
God wanted to win the human race to himself,
so He gave His one and only Son to become a human. Because God's divine nature is united with
human nature in His Son, it's not a stretch to say
that God led us to himself by becoming one of us.
In the same way, if we expect to lead people, we
will have to closely identify with them. Realistic
Expectation No. 12 calls us to be real, to be trans-
parent, so that others can view us as believable.

IT TAKES WILLINGNESS

Some are unwilling to come off the rigid idea
that insists, "I could never be a people person." That's
so sad and so wrong. Yes, it's sad and wrong when

we put more credibility in a temperament test or a personality profile than we do in the God who has asked, "Is anything too hard for me?" (Jer. 32:27). It is God's will that each leader should become a people person. The question is, "Are we willing to allow Him to change us from our stubborn mindsets?" In the words of a real faith hero, my friend, Evangelist Stephen Manley, "Are we willing to turn Jesus loose to live His life of love through us?"

Remember Moses? God wanted him to lead His people out of Egypt, but Moses kept insisting that he had failed all of his public speaking classes in college and it would never work. Mark it down. When God summons a leader, the speech-making is pretty much over. God wants leaders who will fight for Him to free His people. When was the last time you read the account of Moses when he confronted the Pharaoh of Egypt? Take a look at how Moses did after he finally said yes to be God's leader of people. Maybe he stuttered when he tried to speak, but make no mistake about it, Moses became a people person. Once he even told God that if God was not going to help His people, He could kill the leader too. Well, let's not get carried away. We must keep God first, but relating to people is also essential.

If we are willing, God will make us leaders after His own heart. He will transform us into leaders who may have been born timid and introverted, but because of His grace we are now outgoing and overflowing with the good news of our Great God.

LOVER OF PEOPLE

I must confess that at times I've thought more humanly than holy. For example, *loving the Lord my God with all of my heart, mind, soul, and strength* seems much easier than *loving others as I love my-self* (see Mark 12:30-31). Once when I was struggling with caring for people, I asked God to help me by giving me a new vision. He did. In a voice that was not audible but much louder than that, I sensed the Lord saying, "I will help you to see all people from the viewpoint that I saw all people while I was being crucified." Now that's a life-changing perspective. I've never been the same since. I've never looked at people quite the same way either.

So what must we do practically to become lovers of people? One thing we can do is be persons who are willing to initiate conversations with others. As leaders, we cannot avoid people all the time or even most of the time. Granted, I do not believe we should sacrifice our quiet time with God for noisy time with people; however, we must pray for the perfect balance between "God time" and "people time." I believe that the messages I deliver lose power if I do not interact with the people whom God has entrusted me to lead. Availability and visibility reinforces credibility. Yes, many times I struggle with facing people before and after I have delivered God's Word to them. But guess what? The struggle is good for me and good for them. After preaching and teaching, it's time for reaching. When we talk and pray with people one-on-one, the soil of the soul is softened. The success of our harvest is directly related to our saturating with the people before and after the seed has been scattered.

I tell those who lead alongside me, "Never enter a crowd unless you have time to meet and greet them. If you're in a hurry, at the very least, acknowledge the people you pass so they will know they matter to you." Matthew 9:35-37 tells us, "When Jesus saw the crowds, he had compassion on them" (v. 36). If you read the passage, you will see that Jesus took time to teach them about His kingdom and to touch their lives with healing as well. The leader who prays to teach and to touch the people will experience the deep rewards of being an outgoing and overflowing people person for God. Be a people person of compassion. Our friend Deb Harrison gave me the most powerful definition of "true compassion" I've ever heard. She said softly, "True compassion is your pain in my heart."

LOVING NEIGHBORS WITH LIGHT ROLLS

My granddaddy, Lloyd Davis, is with Jesus now, but while he was here on earth, he sure taught me the meaning of being outgoing and overflowing in order to lead others to Christ. Granddaddy was a great cook. His specialty was homemade yeast rolls. He started from scratch the old-fashioned way. It was a daily joy for him to fix his famous bread. Granddaddy called his bread *light rolls*. And that's exactly what they were, because once he had baked a batch, he would set out to distribute them to the whole neighborhood in Jesus' name. Granddaddy helped reinforce within me this mission statement: *Be light! Go shine!* So, with his *light* rolls in paper bags, he would set out to shine Jesus to his neighbors, especially new neighbors that he could surprise with his recipe of practical love.

One day a new professional couple with a small child moved in just across the street from Granddaddy Lloyd. Hurrying to the kitchen, he got a batch of those light rolls ready for delivery. When he knocked on the door, he was treated harshly and immediately turned away. Granddaddy returned home not understanding what had just happened. As the night fell and he prepared for bed with a heavy heart, there was a knock on the back door. Standing there in the dim light was the family of three. They had tears in their eyes and wanted forgiveness for their knee-jerk reaction to Granddaddy's act of kindness. With trembling lips they asked, "Can we still have the light rolls?" With a smile Granddaddy gave them their bread bag. From that day on, the new neighbors made my granddaddy their emergency babysitter. Yes, their only child, a boy, adopted Granddaddy, and Granddaddy adopted him too. He never gave up on his outgoing and overflowing lifestyle. His daily lifestyle was a devoted *light* style.

PREACHING OR PORK CHOPS

Granddaddy Lloyd was born timid and to himself, but the Lord who lived inside him changed Granddaddy into an outgoing and overflowing beacon for His glory and for the good of others. After Granddaddy's death, we found one little, tattered newspaper article in his wallet. The article was actually a story about loving people to the Lord. The story went something like this:

In a certain town there was a preacher and an atheist. The preacher would often stop by and visit with the atheist, trying to talk him toward faith in God. It wasn't working at all. One day the atheist was sick in bed, so after their visit the preacher had to show himself out the front door. As he was leaving, it suddenly dawned on him that there was no heat in the house and it was wintertime. As he passed through the kitchen, out of curiosity, he peeked in the refrigerator. There was no food in it. On the way home the preacher made two stops.

First, he stopped by the coal company and paid for a delivery to the address of the atheist. Second, he went into a supermarket with a delivery service and placed a basic grocery order to be dropped off at the address of the atheist as well. As he left the supermarket, he turned to the clerk and told him to add some pork chops to the list. A week later the preacher received a call from the son of the atheist. The son explained that his father had died but had left a note beside his bed for the preacher. The note was short but sweet. "Tell the preacher that I accepted his Jesus as my own and it wasn't the preaching but the pork chops that won me over."

Outgoing and overflowing leaders are the kind of leaders the Lord deserves and demands. Even if it takes light rolls or pork chops, people who love Jesus and the people for whom He died preach sermons with their very lives.

REALISTIC EXPECTATION No. 11
EMBRACE PASSIONATE CREATIVITY

Is there any greater offense in the universe than a leader who makes the good news of Jesus boring to the people he or she has been entrusted to lead? God is our Creator God, which means He's creative. Genesis tells us that we are made in the image of God, and that must mean that somewhere inside the people He created, God deposited creativity. Creativity to which we can add passion so that God might get glory and people might get God.

BE A SELF-STARTER

One thing I don't quite understand is a believer who has to be jump-started. A car with a dead battery is so annoying. After hooking up the jumper cables two or three times to a dead battery, I make a big decision. Buy a new battery. The same is true when I invite people to lead alongside me on our leadership team. Once they are a part of who we are, they should carry out the vision God has given them with passionate creativity. Creativity is the gift God gives to us, and passion is the gift we give to God. I'm using the word "passion" as a synonym for "desire." God designs us. We desire God. Together we partner with God in the destiny of eternal souls. I call that divine teamwork and love-based leadership.

After I call a leader to join me in divine teamwork with Almighty God, I expect him or her to go to God and go to the people. If that person spends all of his or her time hanging around my office door waiting for direction, we've got a serious issue to address. Once the Lord sounds His call, we become responsible for the stall. Now I don't mean that stillness is wasted time, but I do mean that God has a plan and we must get with Him to work out the details. For example, if I am the lead pastor, and I have to carry out the administrative pastor's responsibility, then one of us needs to go. It's bad stewardship. It can also be very paralyzing for the entire leadership team.

In my opinion, the Lord deserves creative and passionate thoroughbred leaders. There's really no room for irresponsible and stubborn mule-like leaders in the Kingdom. Yes, I know I'm somewhat passionate about yoking up with self-starters. Why? When I'm yoked up with self-starters, I get really creative for my Christ.

MAXIMIZE YOUR GIFTS TO MATCH YOUR CALLING

Passion is about desire. Passion is also about delight. One way to increase creativity is to delight in the One who called you and to delight in the calling He's entrusted to you. Psalm 37:4 is a life verse for me. Hear it from the *New Living Translation* of the Holy Bible: "Take delight in the LORD, and he will give you your heart's desires." It is a verse that's loaded with passion. It begins with delight and ends with desire. If we ever hope to experience spiritual success, we must begin with delight and end with desire.

My wife and I have attended an annual church leaders' conference for years now. We have plans to go again. We delight in the conference because we have seen God all through it. Now some of my colleagues have attended once or twice and have talked themselves out of ever attending again. Perhaps my wife and I have a different perspective. We go seeking God and seeing Him in the people, not just in the curriculum or the agenda. For us, the conference is more than a conference. It's a conversation, a journey, a relationship that God has given to us to help us maximize our gifts to match our calling.

I'm convinced that longevity is the greatest convincer when it comes to experiencing fruit. On a trip to the Holy Land I learned that when a father plants an olive tree, thirty years may pass before it actually bears fruit. Still, he cares for it diligently. He may never directly enjoy the fruit of the tree, but indirectly he is already enjoying fruit in his heart because he knows his children and his grandchildren will be blessed by his perseverance.

As leaders, sometimes we may not realize that the ones we're leading are first and foremost those closest to us—our own children and grandchildren, or other members of our families. My life's goal is to be loved, appreciated, and respected most by the one who calls me Husband and the ones who call me Daddy. There's one particular verse in the Bible that I absolutely seek to make a reality in my own life as a leader. It's Heb. 11:7: "It was by faith that Noah built an ark to save his family from the flood" (NLT).

I wonder how many days Noah felt like giving up. Do you think he ever just wanted to throw in the towel as a leader? Sure he did. Yet, he continued to build the very best ark he could build. He continued to maximize his gifts to match his calling. When the door of the massive boat was closed by God, Noah had not been effective at all in leading his human neighbors to safety, but his whole family showed up on the deck with their suitcases. The neighbors said no to Noah's plea to enter the ark; however, his wife, his sons, and their wives all answered yes to his invitation. Those closest to him were led to safety, and they profited greatly because of his passionate creativity.

Noah was surely fulfilled in his life's calling. He was fulfilled because he had led the one who called him Husband and the ones who called him Daddy to salvation. My guess is that Noah's love for God and his family was much more responsible in winning his wife and sons than was all of his nail pounding, yet the ark had to be built before the blessing of rescue could be given. It took the gift of God's creativity planted in the soul of a willing and passionate man. Noah was willing to maximize his gifts to match God's calling for his life. God was Noah's God, and Noah was God's man. Because Noah partnered with God, the ark was built and the human race was preserved. Indeed, it is correct to say that Noah was a life preserver for his present family and the future world.

RELATIONSHIPS ROCK

Yes, Noah could boast of the world's first floating zoo. That must have given him some measure of satisfaction in life, but the real satisfaction was that his own loved ones had found refuge because of his masterful carpentry and stick-to-itiveness. Noah built an ark for his family. That's action. That's *what Noah did.*

Noah also built his family into the ark. That's attitude. That's *who Noah was*. Knowing that all of his family members were safe on the inside with him, the obedient boat builder experienced forty days and nights of purpose. If old Noah had written his autobiography, what might the title be? Do you think he might have titled it *Relationships Rock*? I like your passionate creativity. Relationships do *rock* the boat—that is, relationships always *anchor* the boat to the Solid Rock.

FOUR

REALISTIC EXPECTATION No. 10
EMBRACE A BALANCED WORK ETHIC

When someone says to me, "I'm a driven person,"
I know for sure that person will not be an asset to
our leadership team. People who label themselves
as driven scare me. It is like owning a vehicle with
two accelerator pedals and no brake pedal. Whenever Christians use the word "driven," I must honestly confess, I get nervous. The word that thrills my
heart is "balance." So naturally, when it is time to
bring new partners aboard our "disciple ship," much
of the interview is spent talking about the realistic
expectation of a *balanced* work ethic. We don't need
workaholics, and we don't want lazybones, either. We
look for real people who have a balanced work ethic.

EMBRACING GOD'S AGENDA

Having a balanced work ethic is not necessarily automatic. It takes a willingness to struggle until

our schedules and priorities are pleasing to God. Finding balance is at the very heart of true godliness. The only way we can embrace God's agenda is to make a spiritual journey to the heart of Jesus.

I have no doubt that Jesus was the most balanced leader ever. I love the story of Jesus found in Mark 1:29-39. Talk about balance. Jesus spent the evening healing large numbers of people and casting out many demons. When morning came, Jesus had already left the town long before daybreak to pray in the wilderness. His disciples, all in a driven panic, came to where He was and said, "Everyone is looking for you!" Jesus replied calmly, "Let us go somewhere else . . . so I can preach" (vv. 37-38). Jesus was a balanced leader. He was talking about balanced ministry. He had healed some of the sick, cast out some evil spirits, spent the morning praying, and now was ready to do some preaching but not until He had enjoyed a nice long walk to another village. Jesus turned His back on being driven, especially when His disciples were trying to force Him into the maddening mold. Jesus did not run after the expectations of others. He was all about embracing His Father's agenda.

THE HEALTHY BALANCED LIFE

My dad is a commercial fisherman. That means he makes most of his living as a shrimp boat captain on and around the Atlantic Ocean. Working on the

water is a hard life. It is more like a calling than a ca-
reer. Dealing with bad weather is one of the most un-
certain challenges associated with life on the sea. One
nine-letter, weather word can wipe out everything a
shrimp boat captain owns: *Hurricane!* A few years
back, a hurricane named Emily was bearing down on
Harkers Island, North Carolina, where my dad lives
and harbors his shrimp boat. A newspaper reporter
from Columbia, South Carolina, photographed my
dad readying his vessel for the storm. When the photo
came out in the newspaper, there was Dad swimming
with ropes in the harbor, securing his boat as best
he could. The boat was separated from the dock at
four points. Yes, one anchor in each direction held
the boat through the hurricane. The balancing hold
of the anchors secured the boat against the storm.

Whenever I think about my dad preparing
his shrimp boat for a hurricane, I think about the
balance I want before, during, and after the life-
threatening hurricanes bear down on me and my
loved ones. My earthly father knows how to get
a hurricane-balanced boat. My Heavenly Father
knows how to give a healthy-balanced life. So I
go to Him for the four anchors that will give to
me a balanced life and a balanced work ethic.

FOUR ANCHORS FOR BALANCE

As I continuously seek my Abba Father for balance, the same four anchors keep offering me balance in all types of weather. If I desire the healthy-balanced life, I must give equal attention to all four ropes and the anchors they are tied to. I find health in my life and balance in my work ethic as I simultaneously look after *adoration, occupation, recreation,* and *restoration.* More simply, if I want health in my life, I must seek God to help me maintain balance between *worship, work, play,* and *rest.* The precious Holy Spirit, my life Counselor, will give me without interruption this healthy balance.

The Anchor of Adoration

If we are ever to be true spiritual leaders, we must be people after God's own heart. We must be worshippers. Worship is more about knowing God than knowing about God. Worship is more about spending time with Him than spinning our wheels for Him. Worship matters to God. Worship is a priority on His agenda, and we will never know balanced lives or balanced work ethics until we embrace Him in worship. Worship is not something we just speed through. It is not a destination thing; worship is a journey thing. Worship is a 24-7 thing, an unending attitude of adoration of the Almighty.

My mentor in life, James Spruill, taught me not to compartmentalize life with secular and sacred labels. God is omnipresent, so whether we're in the sandbox with the little kids, shooting hoops with the teens, or standing behind the pulpit on Sunday morning, all seasons of life are equally sacred. When Jesus said, "Surely I am with you always" (Matt. 28:20), worship certainly became an all-day, every-day, all-night, every-night way of life. Make sure the anchor of adoration is not dragging the bottom in your life, or your balance will be out of whack. The anchor of adoration must be set deep in the Rock at all times.

The Anchor of Occupation

Adoration is worship, and occupation is worship too. However, we need to practically incorporate both worship and work in our lives. Without worship we become workaholics. Without work we become lazybones. Neither alone offers balance that helps us or pleases God. Work is *what we do* in obedience to God's agenda for our lives. Worship is *how we go about doing what we do* in obedience to God's agenda for our lives. Work is about action. Worship is about attitude. Work done in a worshipful way pleases God and balances us.

When I am looking for leaders to partner alongside me in ministry, I ask the question, "How many hours will you work each week?" It's a loaded question. If their lips start moving quickly, I know we are in trouble. Some have answered quickly, saying, "Seventy or eighty hours—that's my style." I pause and then reply, "Well, you won't be working here with that style because you'll cramp my style, and I'm not looking for more false guilt to carry." When it comes to work, the words "realistic expectations" are very, very important. God wants us to work, but He's not a one-anchor God. There are three other anchors that need tending so that our lives will be inwardly balanced and outwardly beautiful. All work and no worship, no play, and no rest make an unbalanced person and an unsuccessful leader.

The Anchor of Recreation

Worship and work are enhanced when we take time to play. Yes, adoration, occupation, and recreation really do go together. Talk about false guilt. Why is it that leaders feel guilty when they take time to play? I'm convinced the enemy spends more time cutting the anchor rope that leads to recreation in the life of the leader more than any other of the four ropes. Why? Because playing, taking time for recreation, is the breeding ground for joy and lightheartedness in our lives. And well, we all know that misery loves company. The devil doesn't want us having what he doesn't have. *Fun!* When we play and have fun we become like little children, and you know what Jesus said about little children: "Unless you change and become like little children, you will never enter the kingdom" (Matt. 18:3).

Starting to make sense, isn't it? If we don't tend to the anchor of recreation, we will miss out on re-creation. Schedule some fun time, some playtime, into your life, and *being driven* will begin to make way for *being balanced.* I promise. If you will begin to schedule in recreation, eventually it will become spontaneous, a holy habit you will refuse to live without. That's a good thing and a God thing too. If you really want to upset the disciples in a good way, just be like Jesus. Take time to play with the children. And don't let that little boy or little girl inside you die. If you already have, cheer up, because our God specializes in resurrections. Ask Him to resurrect recreation in your life. Let the child in you live and laugh again. Ask God to re-create childlike wonder in your life now.

The Anchor of Restoration

Finally, do not forget to set the anchor of rest on solid ground. Remember, we need all four anchors for healthy balance in our lives and our work ethics—adoration, occupation, recreation, and, yes, finally, restoration. I'm convinced that many Christians and especially Christian leaders do not need another sermon. They just need to take a nap. I also know that Jesus wants us to rest. He offers it to us in Matt. 11:28: "Then Jesus said, 'Come to me, all of you who are weary and carry heavy burdens, and I will give you rest'" (NLT).

Is it possible that the four anchors we are talking about are simply and profoundly about giving gifts? Stick with me, now. Is it possible that *worship* and *work* are both gifts we give to God, *play* is a gift we give to ourselves, and *rest* is a gift Jesus gives to us? I think it's possible, indeed. Perhaps the reason we have no rest in our lives is we don't, or won't, come to Jesus to receive His rest as our gift.

The anchor of resting is connected to the rope of trusting. In his journals, Oswald Chambers was once up against some seemingly impossible circumstances. He went to the Lord in prayer and sensed the Lord saying, "Trust me and do the next thing you can do." After some contemplation, Oswald concluded that he would do just that. So he simply trusted God and did the next thing he could do. He took a nap.[1]

Resting is a gift the Lord gives to us so we can learn to trust Him more. Talk about the healthy-balanced life. That's the kind of life I want to live. That's the kind of work ethic I embrace. A work ethic that is beautifully balanced with four faithful anchors—adoration, occupation, recreation, and restoration—will help keep the boat crew from being upset by bad weather reports and unruffled by God's divine interruptions as well. Come hail, high water, or hurricane, these anchors will hold us steady and keep us strong because they are lodged into the Rock of Ages!

So let's shake our fist in faith at the winds and the waves and declare, *Jesus is onboard our boat!*

REALISTIC EXPECTATION No. 9
BE EXTREMELY FLEXIBLE

When I was a kid in the 1960s, there was an afternoon television program starring the clay animation characters Gumby and Pokey. Some of you know just what I am talking about. Our local five-and-dime department store sold toy versions of these characters. They were bendable little fellows made of rubber-coated wire. They were the most flexible toys I ever owned. Maybe they were not exactly safe by today's standards for children's toys, but they sure were fun to bend and stretch! When it comes to choosing leadership partners, I look for the Gumby and Pokey types—people who believe in teamwork and prove it by being extremely flexible, not in message but in methods. When it comes to message, Jesus is the only Way, but when it comes to methods, everyone on our team must admit, "My right answer is probably not the only right answer."

OPPOSITE OF "MY WAY OR THE HIGHWAY" MIND-SETS

Those who possess extreme flexibility have contagious and irresistible mind-sets that are the opposite of "my way or the highway" mind-sets. Extremely flexible people do not stir up competition among the team members but instead instigate inspiration. They embrace new leadership methods wholeheartedly, adapting quickly to whatever inconveniences may affect them personally by making needed adjustments that accompany seasons of change.

Maybe you are just waiting to hear it bluntly? OK, here it is plain, simple, and direct. Leadership teams die on the vine when control freaks take over. Always having to be in control is one of the most evident masks for fear that wannabe leaders too often wear. Having to be in charge is not a sure sign that someone is smart. It is more often a dead giveaway that someone is scared. When it comes to fearless leading, *letting go* is just as important as *holding on*. In the words of an old Kenny Roger's country-western song, real, effective leaders "know when to hold 'em" and they also "know when to fold 'em." Yes, real, effective leaders know *when* to fight and *when* to surrender too. Knowing when to flex and when to be flex-

ible are both essential to strong leadership. Knowing
when to retreat is a key to knowing how to advance.

HILLS TO DIE ON

The longer I lead, the shorter my list of
"hills to die on" gets. As an extremely flexible
leader, one of my major mottoes for living is this:
I must be willing to lose a few personal battles
that we might win the all-out war for souls.

Come to think of it, Jesus only died on one hill—
the hill called Mount Calvary. Jesus died on one hill
and He died for one reason. He did not die to start
a new religion. Jesus died on the hill called Mount
Calvary to make relationships new between Holy
God and sinful people. Nailed to the Cross, Jesus
certainly modeled extreme flexibility as the Leader
of all leaders. How did He model extreme flexibility?
Jesus won us by losing himself. The religious leaders mocked Jesus with these words, "He saved others,
. . . but he can't save himself" (Matt. 27:42). Exactly.
That was the hill He chose to die on. The Son of God
knew He could not save himself and save us too. So
He profoundly chose to save us on Friday and simply trusted His Sunday resurrection to His Father.

As leaders, while we are deliberating over which
hills we will die on, let us not forget that Jesus, the
Greatest Leader ever, did not die on *hills*, He just died
on *one hill*. As His life ebbed away, He modeled true

[handwritten margin note: What a model: We surrender today for God to Resurrect tomorrow]

servant leadership. Servant leadership is very attractive to a world that is sadly accustomed to seeing leaders who want *to be served* rather than *to serve.* When we model extreme flexibility, we indeed provide undeniable proof to a watching world that genuine servant leadership is underway on our watch as leaders.

CAPTAIN BILLY

As a teen, I worked summer after summer on my dad's shrimp boat. It was like a rite of passage for any male child with our family name, Willis. My dad knew that I would at best only be a boy hired to do a man's job. Still, he did not steal my dignity when I became a greenhorn mate on the deck of his fishing vessel. Quite the contrary, Dad proved his character to me instead.

To everyone else around the docks, my dad was Captain Billy. To me he was Daddy, and a loving daddy in every sense of the word. From day one, I got a full mate's share when payday rolled around. I did not get a full share of the profits because I earned a full share. I got a full share because my dad, Captain Billy, pulled his weight as captain and most of my weight as mate as well. None of the other hired men ever questioned my pay, because my dad, their captain, outserved all of us combined. It's how he led his crew.

My dad has always been a hero to me, and he always will be. The reasons are many, but none greater than the fact that he modeled servant leadership. As a result, I could see Christ in his lifestyle. Even though he was the captain, he proved to be extremely flexible, taking on the form of a deckhand to save face for his teenage son who was trying to become a man. I needed a strong hand to become a man, and Captain Billy, my daddy, provided his strong, serving hands to make it happen. I am so grateful that my dad was willing to leave his captain's chair and join me on the deck of that old shrimp boat. As he did so, he simply but profoundly said, "I believe in you, my son, and I'm willing to come down the ladder to meet you at the bottom rung."

RELIGION OR RELATIONSHIP

The doorbell sounded at our home. One look through the window and I thought to myself, *I really don't have time for this. Or do I?* Two young, religious boys dressed in Sunday slacks, white shirts, and ties were waiting for me. I opened the door with a gentle smile. Their name tags introduced the door knockers as elders. I simply said, "I'm Kerry." I let them share everything they wanted to share, listening with great respect to every word and praying under my breath for their seemingly set minds and hearts. When my turn finally came to speak, I told them I admired their zeal and perseverance for their religion, but I was not interested in a religion, just a relationship. They seemed puzzled, but curious. Then they asked almost in unison the seeking question that always makes my soul smile: "What's the difference between religion and a relationship?"

I sweetly and calmly attempted to disarm them as I carefully and prayerfully chose each word, explaining that I, like them, had also once been very religious, but religion had left me cold and confused. As a result, now I was only interested in a relationship with Jesus. My closing statement made one of the young men obviously nervous and caused the other young man to just sort of stare at me. His eyes seemed to be saying, "I'm hearing what you're saying, sir." My closing statement of hope was this truth I suddenly recalled from a mission class many years ago in Bible college: "Religion is when we climb our own ladders of good works thinking we will somehow meet God at the top, but a relationship is realizing that God already came down the ladder in the person of His Son, Jesus, to meet us at the bottom rung."

With that, the nervous, lead elder turned to leave while the tenderer young missionary seemed be experiencing a genuine burning in his bosom. He seemed to hold on to my every word. As the young dedicated but misdirected men left my front porch, I prayed that a godly heartburn would cause genuine heart-turn and that they would come to desire an intimate and personal relationship with Jesus. How sad it would be for them to just spend their whole lives in an empty, ladder-climbing religious pursuit.

So, what does extreme flexibility have to do with this story? Plenty. On the one hand, religion is cold, extremely rigid, a slow but sure freezing of the heart. Religion is usually just a mask made by people to hide insecurity and to promote fear. On the other hand, a relationship is warm, extremely flexible, a melting of the heart. A relationship is always a God-given invitation to love and to be loved. To paraphrase a great verse in the Bible, "Perfect love drives away all tormenting fear" (1 John 4:18).

Let us be warm, relationship-focused leaders, extremely flexible people who embrace servant leadership and in so doing lead others away from rigid and frigid religion.

REALISTIC EXPECTATION No. 8
EMBRACE A GREEN-APPLE ATTITUDE

After an apple turns red, there's only one stage left. Fall off the tree and rot. However, a green apple is always growing. Surely, it is a realistic leadership expectation to be ever growing, always learning. I call it a green-apple attitude.

As a young boy, I must admit that I owned a few records by the Beatles. Records were to my generation what MP3 players are to this generation—a way to listen to music. Anyway, I still like the Beatles' music. You want to know why? I'm a drummer. Yes, I was young and now I am older, but I still play a five-piece Pearl drum set. I guess I'm just an old hippie! Well, on those old Beatles' records I owned, there was an unforgettable graphic stuck to each one.

Guess it was a logo of sorts for the record company. The logo was a big, green apple. It's unforgettable.

Leaders who are marked by the green-apple attitude are unforgettable too. Like the Beatles, people with green-apple attitudes never go out of style. Lifelong learners are always cool, man.

LIFELONG LEARNERS

My spiritual mentor, James, is about twenty years older than me, his spiritual protégé, but we are both still green apples. James calls it, "Not being dead from the neck up." Our relationship must have the DNA of a Paul and Timothy relationship. We are both committed to being lifelong learners of our Lord Jesus. Though James lives outside of Nashville, and I live in Virginia's Shenandoah Valley, class is always in session between us whether we're on the phone or exchanging e-mails with one another. Many times our conversations begin and end by sharing what we have learned most recently. We get together face-to-face as often as possible and recently taught at a church convention as a green-apple tag team. It was wonderful. Indeed, ours is a great, sharing relationship that certainly humbles me and hopefully honors God.

If you have moved beyond being a green apple, this message from another old song by the Beatles is appropriate: "Get back, get back! Get back to where you once belonged!" When we stop learning, we stop living and start dying. Let us learn from the red apple and not fall off the tree prematurely. If we do, the certain scenario of rotting is our only option.

CHILDLIKE WONDER AND IMAGINATION

Can you imagine Jesus with the little children? Sometimes as adult followers of our Lord, we seem to lose the wonder as we worship Him. I think a great definition of pure worship is *a wonder-full cleansing of the imagination*. As Jesus spent time with the little children, two things had to thrill His heart— their wonder and their imagination. I once heard a children's pastor, Mark, say that he loved serving little children, because too often adults are hard like cement, they need to be chiseled; teens are stiff like putty, maybe you can mold them; but children are always like sponges, ready to soak up everything you offer them. Childlike wonder and imagination are ideal attitudes for all student types, especially for those of us who purpose to be green-apple leaders for life.

One night as I was tucking our little girl in bed, I knelt beside her for bedtime prayers. After I prayed, I could only hear Allison faintly mumbling, so I said, "Sis, I can't hear your prayer." With appropriate sarcasm, she interrupted her mumbling long enough to address her earthly father: "Duh, dad. I'm not praying to you." I laughed at my little girl's rapid response,

but I also learned from her imaginative approach
to prayer. It was a green-apple moment, for sure.

As leaders, let us approach leadership with a
child's approach. Let us not forfeit wonder or sacrifice
inspiration by getting lost in the details. Wonder and
imagination are our friends. They both lead us like
children—to love and to live like Jesus. At Disneyland,
the theme park engineers are called imagineers. It's
a commitment not to lose the childlike wonder that
gave us such adorable characters as Mickey Mouse,
Donald Duck, and Goofy. How boring life would
be without imagineers and wonder-full leaders.

LOVE TO LEARN AND LEARN TO LOVE

As leaders with green-apple attitudes, our learning must consist of much more than a book-smart
quest for knowledge alone. That would be a tragic
end. If we embrace only a *loving to learn* and somehow forget *learning to love,* all our learning will
be meaningless. If the lecture of our lives is titled
"Learning," then the laboratory of our lives is called
Loving. What we know is not an end in itself. Who
we know is. In fact, who we know is the heart of our
journey and the pinnacle of our destination as well.

In Matt. 7:21-23, the *New Living Translation*
records these powerful words of Jesus as He is bringing His Sermon on the Mount to a screeching halt:

Not everyone who calls out to me, "Lord! Lord!" will enter the Kingdom of Heaven. Only those who actually do the will of my Father in heaven will enter. On judgment day many will say to me, "Lord! Lord! We prophesied in your name and cast out demons in your name and performed many miracles in your name." But I will reply, "I never knew you. Get away from me, you who break God's laws."

Jesus makes it quite clear that His true disciples need more than knowledge for the sake of knowledge. As true disciples of the Lord, we must know Him; more specifically, we must be known by Jesus. It's not enough to love to learn about Jesus. We must learn to love and know Jesus, personally.

THE COMMANDER IN CHIEF

It was a rainy, December day, but my spirit would not be dampened. Our family of four had tickets to celebrate and commemorate the hundred-year anniversary of Orville and Wilbur Wright's first flight at the Wright Brothers Memorial in Kitty Hawk, North Carolina. I parked our car and we boarded one of the shuttle buses. As we rode toward the site, a rumor was in the air. President George W. Bush was expected to make a surprise visit at the festivities.

Late in the morning, after a failed attempt by reenactors to fly a model glider in the same fashion Orville and Wilbur had a hundred years earlier, a roar could be heard across the sky. Sure enough, four Marine helicopters circled and landed. It was impressive. The door opened and out came the commander in chief. No matter what your political preference, if you are a red, white, and blue American citizen and you've never seen an American president in person, take it from me, you will be impressed when he or she makes his or her arrival. I'm sure of it. I've been there and done that.

President Bush took the stage next to the famous actor and airplane enthusiast John Travolta, the emcee of the celebration. I stood in awe as I watched with my very own eyes the president of the United States of America make a very inspiring speech about two great American pioneer leaders—Orville and Wilbur Wright. Talk about two green-apple attitude leaders! The Wright Brothers never lost their childlike approach. When all other boys became young men, they gave up their wonder of flying as silly childhood fantasy. However, when the Wright Brothers became young men, they never lost their childhood wonder and imagination of flying. Instead it became their heartbeats. Every time I board a commercial jet, I am so thankful that the Wright Brothers made every boy's flying fantasy an actual reality for the whole world.

Well, the commander in chief completed his visit with us and waved good-bye from the little Kitty Hawk airstrip as his flying machine, a chopper, lifted off and away. As I reflect back on that soggy but inspiring day, I realize that over the years I've learned much about Orville and Wilbur Wright, President George W. Bush, and even John Travolta, but I don't really know any of them personally. They don't know me either. But then again, these men are only leaders that I admire. Guess what? When it comes to the God-Man that I adore, the Leader that I really love to learn about and I have really learned to love, Jesus Christ, I do know Him and He does know me. Actually, His Spirit lives within me. We are real close. I'm not merely Jesus obsessed. It's much better than that. I'm mainly Jesus possessed.

One day, the physical Jesus will make His final approach in the clouds, and according to John 14:3, He's coming back to get me and to take me so I can be with Him forever! When Jesus returns, if I'm still alive on planet earth, I'm confident He will find faith on the earth. Yes, as He arrives, if I'm still alive, I plan to have faith, growing faith, still going on in my own life.

I'm not sure what Jesus will say when He physically returns to get me, but I'm thinking of two words that seem pretty appropriate for me to shout as He makes His descent: "Relationships rule!" And who knows, in heaven, I might just sing a remake of an old Beatles' classic for my Jesus: "Eight days a week, I'll love You, love You, love You." And I'm pretty sure that even in heaven, especially in heaven, the green-apple logo will still be spinning on the turntable of my soul. Surely, there will be plenty more learning and loving happening there.

REALISTIC EXPECTATION No. 7
EMBRACE A GOD-CAN FAITH

Two of the early words our young son, Grayson, sang out were, "God can!" He picked the words up from a recorded children's musical that he listened to when he went to bed at night. Born with some medical unknowns, Grayson's two little words of vibrant faith, *God can*, spoke volumes to his young, first-time parents. I can see him now in our backyard tree swing. As I pushed him wildly, I asked, "Who can?" Laughing out of control, he sung back his undeniable two-word answer in rapid repetition, "God can! God can! God can!"

I love being surrounded by leadership partners who embrace a can-do spirit. A faith that personally believes and publicly declares, "Our God can do all things," is very attractive and very encouraging.

God-can faith inspires authentic happiness. That's why the hymn writer penned these words: "Trust and obey, / For there's no other way / To be happy in Jesus / But to trust and obey."[1] When we really trust God, obeying Him is much simpler and heart happiness in inevitable. So who can lead us through seemingly impossible circumstances? God can!

AND TRUST HIM

If you've ever left one of your children at a summer camp for a week or at a college campus for a school year, you know the heart-wrenching pain of being a loving parent. Awhile back, our family of four left home on a hot August morning for a 441-mile trip to Mount Vernon, Ohio. Our son, Grayson, was beginning his freshman year at the Nazarene university there. Our hearts were troubled. I had no idea how my wife; our sixteen-year-old daughter, Allison; and I would ever make the trip home without our eighteen-year-old son.

After moving Grayson's things into Oakwood Hall, the freshman dorm, we went for a Chinese buffet lunch and then back to the college chapel for the closing service. As the worship leader led us in choruses and hymns, I was pretty much an emotional wreck and a spiritual basket case. We struggled through the song "Here I Am to Worship," and all I could think about was Abraham. As part of his worship, he walked his son, Isaac, up to Mount Moriah, and as part of Kerry's worship, I had driven my son, Grayson, up to Mount Vernon.

One of my life verses is Gal. 2:20. As the freshmen service took place, the chapel seat I was sitting in was seat No. 220. The *New International Version* of Gal. 2:20 is, "I have been crucified with Christ and I no longer live, but Christ lives in me. The life I live in the body, I live by faith in the Son of God, who loved me and gave himself for me." The verse never felt more real to me than at that chapel service. Especially, the part that declares, "And I no longer live."

As I questioned God in my heart, asking, "How will I ever survive this?" the answer came in the singing of the next song, an old hymn of the church that has been like a soundtrack loop for my life as a pastor. Yes, as we were singing "I Surrender All," this line reinforced my hope: "I will ever love *and trust Him*."[2] For some reason, I had never paid much attention to those three words strung together, "and trust Him." Suddenly, my soul began to breathe again. Indeed, I cried as we said good-bye, and yes, I admit I even slept with my son's favorite ESPN T-shirt many nights afterward. Yes, I survived and continue to survive physical separation from my only son by exercising a *God-can faith* and by repeating these seven words over and over: "I will ever love *and trust Him*."

Pray for me, because my only daughter leaves soon for college as well. What will I do? Ever loving and trusting God remains my tried-and-true, tested hope handle.

BIG-HONKIN' HOPE AND SUPERSIZED FAITH

As leaders, we must communicate three words that the world desperately needs to know: "Hope is alive!" And hope has a name—*Jesus*. By "big-honkin' hope," I mean precisely this: The hope we have in Jesus must not only be whispered to our seemingly hopeless world but must also be shouted out loud with big-honkin' horns when necessary. How will the seemingly hopeless know that hope is alive and hope has a name unless we proclaim the message from the rooftops? They won't. As leaders, it must be part of our jubilant, joyous descriptions to make sure those among us, those around us, and those beyond us hear the Good News. Faith comes by hearing about hope!

We live in a supersized society. Burger joints offer supersized meals. Department stores offer supersized price cuts. If soft drink cups get any bigger, one hazard of driving could be death by drowning as we're trying to drink our supersized colas. It seems that we have supersized expectations for everything these days.

Talk about supersized expectations, it's getting ridiculous. On our way home from vacation, my wife,

Kim, and I stopped at a traffic light. A white school
bus pulled alongside us. The seats were not occupied
by schoolchildren but by furry canines. I'm serious.
The bus driver was transporting dogs. The words on
the bus advertised "Paws Pet Resort, with daily pick-
up and delivery of our four-legged friends." Kim and I
laughed for miles. You heard it here first, folks, doggy
day care now offers school bus service. Kim and I
agreed that we would not let our hyper beagle pup,
Oreo, know about this supersized service for man's
best friend. He might get some unrealistic expectations about his future. Besides, he has some Jack
Russell in his genes, and the dog experts say if you
mix beagle with Jack Russell you get a pup that can
only be described with four words: "Extremely intel-
ligent. Wreaks havoc!" A dog as smart as ours doesn't
need school or a school bus. We already have to spell
certain words in his presence. He's that smart.

The point is, if people can have supersized expectations for their pets that include school bus trans-
portation, then surely we as fully devoted followers of
Jesus can have supersized expectations for the kind
of faith the leaders we partner with possess. As leaders, we can learn much about trusting God with true,
supersized faith by reading, reflecting, and refocusing
our lives according to Heb. 11, the Holy Bible's hall
of faith. Verse 6 is a great place to saturate our souls
for a while: "It is impossible to please God without

faith. Anyone who wants to come to him must believe that a God exists and that he rewards those who sincerely seek him" (NLT). Such is the definition of supersized heroes of the faith. When it comes to faith, let's make it supersized, fiery, and vibrant.

RISKY FAITH FELLS GIANTS

On my last trip to the Holy Land I stood on the faith-inspiring, sacred ground where 1 Sam. 17 happened. The place is known as the Valley of Elah. The great, faith extravaganza that took place there spotlighted a weekend warrior named David and a battle champion named Goliath. God called David, "a man after my own heart" (Acts 13:22). I believe David's genuine worship of God partially qualified him to be a man after God's own heart, and his risky faith in God completed his qualifications. David was a young man who loved and trusted his God. He was for sure a faith-inspiring leader.

After the four of us finished our picnic lunch under a shade tree at the Valley of Elah, Steve, my prayer partner, and I asked our dear friends, devoted guides, and missionary heroes of the faith in their present lives, Lindell and Kay Browning, if we could walk the field of faith for a while. It was very hot, but I was on a mission. I was in search of five faith reminders, and 1 Sam. 17:40 was my treasure map: "He [David] picked up five smooth stones from a stream and put them into his shepherd's bag. Then, armed only with his shepherd's staff and sling, he started across the valley to fight [Goliath]" (NLT).

I went from one side of the Valley of Elah to the other and guess what? I found the streambed. It was dry in August, but smooth stones were every-where. I picked up five, two of which were shaped like hearts. I also picked up ten more smooth stones, five each for my two younger brothers who are also pastors. Talk about original, awe-inspiring, and inexpensive Christmas gifts for leaders.

Some may ask why five smooth stones mean so much to me. It's a good question, but in my opin-ion it's a question that a risky leader with fiery, vi-brant, God-can faith would never ask. Why? Because risky leaders know that risky faith needs every re-minder it can get. That's why the five smooth stones from the Holy Land streambed are so important to me. They serve as one more powerful reminder that inspires me toward risky-faith leadership.

Every time I see or even think about the five smooth stones from the valley stream, I remember the story of the shepherd-boy leader. He was employed primarily as a shepherd for his father, Jesse, and only a part-time soldier in Saul's National Guard. He may have been only a part-time warrior for the king, but he was a full-time worshiper of the King of Kings. David was also a big-time man of faith, willing to risk *anything* to make God *everything* in the eyes of both his people and his enemies. David proved once and for all on that sacred day that risky faith fells giants.

Whenever I think of the God-loving and God-trusting leader David running down the ridge to meet the Philistine champion in the valley, my heart is strangely warmed and my faith is extremely encouraged. As he loaded his slingshot with a smooth stone from the streambed, I'm not sure of everything David was thinking, but moments later as he pulled the fallen giant's sword from its sheath and decapitated Israel's intimidator, I envision David holding the giant's sword in one hand and the giant's head in the other and shouting back toward God's people in rapid repetition, "God can! God can! God can!"

REALISTIC EXPECTATION No. 6
BE A LOVER OF LAUGHTER

I once heard an evangelist say, "Laughter allows
me release to go on as I go all out to reach lost
souls."[1] No doubt, laughter is a gift from God and
those who lead alongside me have to be committed to making laughter their center of gravity.

FUNNY LITTLE DANCES ARE OPTIONAL

I miss my Granny Margery so very much and
seemingly every single day. She grew sweeter with
every passing moment, and her secret was her Lord,
His love, and holy laughter. There is only one way
I could ever describe her in one word: "delightful!"
Now Granny was not born with an angelic voice,

but when laughter is one of your core values, you can still sing and pull it off while you pull others up. That's just what she did. Almost every time she saw my face, she would start singing. I can hear her now singing her classic funny song to me: "Oh round-faced owl, you look so wise, / with that big head and those big eyes. / I bet you never ever knew / a word to say except, 'tahoot, tahoo!'" When I enter heaven some day, I will not be surprised if the Lord sends Granny to the gate to greet me. If He does, I'm sure she'll be doing her funny little dance and singing her second favorite song: "I knew you'd come in the very nick of time. Ho! Ho! Ho! Ho!"

The point is, life on earth is much too short to be sour all the time. People need *sweet* in their lives, not just sour. People want to laugh and people need to laugh. If we claim to be fully alive leaders, we must be lovers of laughter. There's no other option, friends. So take my Granny's example and make it your own. Laughter is not copyrighted, so we can laugh without permission from anyone. We must know how to laugh with others, and in most cases we will probably need to lead the laughter. After all, leaders lead! When it comes to being relational leaders, we cannot say no-no to laughter anymore. We may just need to do our funny little dances and bellow out, "Ho! Ho! Ho! Ho!" OK, funny little dances are optional, if you insist.

MY GRANDDADDY'S FUNERAL

After a long life, my Granddaddy Lloyd passed away. A well-intentioned nurse wanted to shock him back to breathing with electric paddles, but Granddaddy had made us promise earlier that when he drew his final breath, we would not rob him of being with Jesus in eternity by bringing him back to earth. So with his eyes set on eternity, we cried around the hospital bed, but soon our tears would turn into wonderful joy. Well, actually our tears turned into wild laughter. Where? At the funeral home. You have to hear this story. Really, you do.

My granddaddy went to be with Jesus before my grandma did. Now, my grandma is not to be confused with my granny. *Grandma* Irene was a different woman altogether than my *Granny* Margery. I loved them both, but believe me when I say, "They were as different as midnight and midday in so many ways." Anyway, after Granddaddy drew his final breath in the hospital bed, our cries of sorrow very quickly turned to sighs of laughter when our family went to Bell-Munden Funeral Home to watch and to listen as Grandma made arrangements for Granddaddy's send-off. You see, Grandma Irene was a self-proclaimed cheapskate. She hovered over the finances as long as they were married. Granddaddy was a generous man, but up until he could barely move, he mowed yards so he could have a little bit of cash to call his own and to spend on others as he pleased. Once, Grandma Irene had the nerve to go to the bank and remove Granddaddy's name from their joint bank account. At age eighty, Granddaddy threatened to move back in with *his folks* if she didn't reverse the bad decision. Lucky for her, before he got all of his suitcases packed, Grandma got herself back to the bank and made things right.

Anyway, as Grandma planned for Granddaddy's funeral service, she sat in front of the funeral director as the rest of us sat behind her on the couch. She didn't really ask us to come, but we would not have missed it for the world—we wanted to see the big spender go for the gold. Ha. About five minutes into the meeting, Grandma made it plain that she wanted the bare necessities. If the funeral home had provided cheap Styrofoam caskets, she may have purchased one for Granddaddy. As the funeral director tried to keep a straight face, the rest of us were about to wet ourselves holding in our laughter. Somehow we all survived it without rolling off the couch and onto the floor of the funeral parlor. It was a miracle of sorts. Finally, we did somehow convince Grandma to buy Granddaddy a nice, new suit to be buried in. She didn't want to, but we were insisting, so she gave in. Now it seemed that Granddaddy had not owned a nice, new suit in twenty years. I'm not sure. Twenty may be an exaggeration. Perhaps it was more like thirty.

At the funeral, one of the funniest men I ever met came up to the casket to pay his respects to Granddaddy. He was a dear man who had grown up with Granddaddy. They had fished the waters of the Atlantic Ocean together and shared many gut-busting rounds of laughter. When the friend thought the family was out of earshot, I heard him say something like this, "Well, Lloyd, at least you finally got a nice, new suit. You never looked better!" I nearly went into convulsions. It was the funniest thing I had ever heard anyone say to a corpse. Up in glory somewhere, I just knew my granddaddy was jumping up and down with Jesus at this very appropriate humor. Yes, even at his funeral, especially at his funeral.

Real people laugh when life is funny wherever they may be. For our family, Granddaddy's passing literally proved Scripture to be quite true: "Weeping may endure for a night, but joy comes in the morning" (Ps. 30:5, NKJV). Yes, we did some crying, but we also laughed wildly at Granddaddy's funeral. It's called *being real.*

YOU CAN'T BE SERIOUS

When we say we are committed to being leaders who laugh, we are actually committing to the very thing that is most attractive to others—being real. Real people cry. Real people laugh. You will never convince me that Jesus was not the most *real* human being to walk this earth. You will never convince me that Jesus did not laugh. Scripture records the tears of our Lord, but just go ahead and read between the lines. Jesus also laughed His head off at times. It may be out of context, but when Jesus said to the religious boys, "Get the two-by-four out of your own eye and then you might be able to see good enough to remove the sawdust from your brother's eye" (Luke 6:42, author's paraphrase), it strikes me as very funny. Actually, come to think of it, it strikes me as totally hilarious!

Now I have personally been a pastor for over fifteen years. During this time of leadership, it's safe to say that I have indeed done my share of crying, but I must also confess that I have surely done more than my share of laughing. Church people are very funny, and a few are totally hilarious. One day I hope to write the most real book you'll ever read about my life as a pastor, but I have to wait for a few people to go on to glory first. The theme of my sometime-in-the-future best seller might be something like, "If being a pastor doesn't kill you, it will surely make you stronger." I know the crying part of ministry rips your heart out at times. I also know the laughing part of ministry revives your heart all the time.

Listen up, leader. This next statement is grave-yard serious: "You can't be serious all the time!" If you are, your leadership is in serious trouble. Get together with some really humorous people fast before it's too late. They're easy to find. According to Brother John Maxwell, who helped affirm me early on to be a leader who loves laughter, these people are already laughing at you for being so serious. Where are these laughing people? Well, if you happen to be a preacher, you will likely find most of them laughing their heads off in the restroom at the church imme-diately following your serious-only Sunday sermons. Here's another hint. Have you ever noticed how all of a sudden it gets really quiet when you are the last one to enter the board meeting room? Your leader-ship team may have just lightened their load at your expense. They may have just shared something that is totally hilarious about you. Join in the laughter with the others, because I'm pretty sure Jesus already has.

Want to be a really beloved leader? Be will-ing to laugh at yourself and invite the rest of us to laugh at you and your idiosyncrasies too. Besides, we're about to burst a gut holding our laughter in when we're around you. Being a lover of laughter is a quality that is nearly unbeatable, especially for a leader who truly values relationships.

REALISTIC EXPECTATION No. 5
EMBRACE A LIFESAVER MENTALITY

Indeed, I am grateful to be the son *of* a fisherman and a fisherman *for* the Son. Part of my gratitude has to do with the favor of being born and raised near the ocean. As a result of being raised the son, grandson, and great-grandson of fishermen, I have great appreciation for, and gain awesome inspiration from, lighthouses and especially lifesavers.

FRIEND OF SINKERS

If I could relive my life, I think I would sign up to serve at least a few years in the United States Coast Guard. Saving lives is surely the most rewarding calling known to humankind. Recently, I encountered a young coastguardsman in an airport. He had just completed boot camp. I stopped him to tell him he was already a hero in my book. Then I asked him if he knew the motto of those who preceded the U.S. Coast Guard, those who served in the U.S. Lifesaving Service? He wasn't sure, so I gave him the motto as we rode the escalator: "The book says we have to go out. It doesn't say anything about coming back."

Is that an awesome motto or what? Those are the kinds of people I want on the leadership team with me. People who are willing to lay down their lives for others inspire my heart. It's a Jesus thing. Those who serve in the Coast Guard are friends of sinkers. Jesus is the friend of sinners. As a matter of fact, if Jesus had stayed in the tomb long enough to get a tombstone, I'm sure the epitaph would have been just three words, "Friend of Sinners." The hymn "Love Lifted Me" also hints that Jesus could be called a friend of sinkers. It's all about a lifesaving mentality.

WHAT GOD'S WILL IS NOT

Sometimes it may be easier to discover what God's will is by knowing what God's will is not. That's kind of the approach of 2 Pet. 3:9: "He is patient with you, not wanting anyone to perish, but everyone to come to repentance." In other words, God is not willing for one single, solitary soul to be eternally lost. Whatever God wants, He does not want that.

I often carry a film clip around in my briefcase from the movie *Titanic*. The clip shows many people drowning in the freezing waters of the Atlantic while the crew of lifeboats that are half full refuse to risk their own lives to save those who are sinking. Finally, one crewman steers a lifeboat to the freezing and dying people, only to find them already frozen and dead. These horrible words can be heard from the lips of the would-be lifesaver: "We waited too long!"

As leaders, every sinking soul must matter to us. Why? *The book says we have to go out. It doesn't say anything about coming back.* It is not God's will that we only focus on the *found*, when the *lost* need our immediate attention. I often say to our local lifesaving team: "Don't ever forget what it felt like to be lost." God forbid that we would ever forget the sinking hopelessness of being lost. If we do, we will also most tragically forget what God's will is not. We must not adopt a museum mind-set. We must possess the mind-set of activated lifesavers. *All out for souls* must be our mission.

BEFORE IT'S TOO LATE

I remember one particular evening on that humble island I call home. I was six years old. It was a Wednesday evening. Earlier in the week, my mom had received Jesus as her *Life Savior,* and she was as excited as I had ever seen her. I wasn't sure what exactly had happened to my mom, but I was pretty sure it was something really good. As if we were about to be late for a very important date, she loaded my infant brother, Billy Joe, and me into the family car. She pulled out of the driveway and headed toward the east end of the little island we lived on. In a few minutes we were turning left down the Ferry Dock Road and pulling on to the dirt parking lot of the Free Grace Church. As darkness fell, she gathered my brother in her arms and grabbed me by the hand and headed for the church doors. Every once in a while my feet hit the ground.

Inside the vestibule, old saints were gathered, and when we entered, they commenced to shouting praises. Good news travels fast on a coastal island, and the word was out that Mom had been saved. As I stood there wide-eyed and awestruck, Mom's face was lit up like a lighthouse beacon. Once we settled into the pew, Brother Oliver, leader of the meeting, called on my newly converted mom to lead in public prayer. Her prayer was simple, but her final request before her Amen made a powerful impact on me: "Lord," she pled, "help us to reach the lost before it's too late."

The service ended and we were back in our Pontiac. In the darkness, Mom's face was illuminated by the dashboard lights. As I sat and stared, I asked, "Mom, who is lost?" As only a mother could answer, she explained to me that anyone who has not received Jesus as their personal Savior is lost. Skeptics may say it's not possible, but in that mo-

ment I understood what she meant. I understood
that I, too, was lost because I had not asked Jesus
into my heart. It would be a whole seven years later
before I called on Christ to save me from my sins
and the darkness associated with being lost, but on
that Wednesday night, at age six, the Savior made it
plain through my newly saved mom that He wanted
to be my Life Savior, too, and before it was too late.

A SENSE OF URGENCY

Ever since my mom wept and prayed her first
public prayer at the Free Grace Church, I have
had a lifesaver mentality. Yes, from early in my
life, I have known a mind-set of urgency that believes lost people must be reached before it's too
late. Surely I have a sense of urgency for souls, not
to be confused with a state of panic. Prayer produces urgency. Prayerlessness produces panic.

My mom, Melba Ruth Davis Willis, helped in-
still this sense of urgency in me. Yes, it began on
that first Wednesday night when she prayed aloud
at church and then explained it all to me in the Pontiac on the way home. However, it didn't stop there.
Mom carried her burden home with her. To this
day, she still weeps and prays for those who are lost.
She prays that we will reach them before it's too
late. Some people claim to be prayer warriors, but
one thing I believe, real people of prayer won't call

themselves prayer warriors. Others, however, will give them such titles. My mom is a prayer warrior. If she passes the line of worlds before I do, I will convince both of my younger brothers that only two words need to be on her headstone: "She prayed."

People who have real urgency in their hearts for lost people prove their urgency by persistent and passionate prayer lives. To the souls-focused saint, to breathe is to pray. It's more than a panic-stricken, religious activity. It's an ever-urgent, relational attitude.

WHAT'S WRONG WITH YOUR MOM?

At the west end of Harkers Island, our little neighborhood was and still is called Red Hill. Even though Madge and Tommy actually knocked the hallowed hill down to build their house, we still call the area that surrounds John's Creek, Red Hill. On Red Hill, Mom and Dad raised three boys and helped in raising many of the other neighborhood boys too. We had the biggest backyard in the neighborhood. It was good for basketball and baseball, but it was especially great for football. After Dad put up a clothesline for Mom at midfield, we even started kicking field goals. Andy Scott had the best foot around. One day he kicked an extra point right through the bathroom window. The funny part is, Dad was in the bathroom at the time. Well, at least it was extremely funny to us boys. Dad may disagree.

I was raised when parents locked their kids out of the house, not in the house. Now, those were the days. Just before locking us out, Mom would tell me, "Kerry, don't come to the door unless it's an emergency." I knew what that meant. She would be alone with God in the front bedroom passionately praying that lost people would be found before it was too late. One hot day, I approached the door with all of the neighborhood boys in tow. It was an emergency. We were about to die from heatstroke, and we all knew Mom had some cold cherry-flavored Kool-Aid in the fridge. After excessive banging on the back door, Mom finally opened it. I can see her even now. Her hair was smashed. Her eyes were puffy. Her face was red. After several glasses of icy Kool-Aid, one of the boys asked me a confusing question: "Kerry, what's wrong with your mom?"

Honestly, I had no earthly idea what he was talking about. On that day, I started to realize a heavenly truth. My mom was abnormal in a wonderful kind of way. I had taken for granted that all mothers were praying mothers. Obviously, my friend's confusing question placed me on a reality-check journey about that idea. Later in life, I came to understand that I had been given much more than many boys. I had been given a *prayer warrior* mom. And God's Word says, "When someone has been given much, much will be required" (Luke 12:48, NLT).

A few years ago, I called my mom and asked her a simple question: "Mom, what did you primarily pray in that front bedroom?" "Well," Mom said, "mainly I just prayed two prayers over and over. (1) Lord, make *something* out of my three boys. (2) Help us reach the lost before it's too late." Mom admitted that she never thought the Lord would answer her prayer for the lost by making something out of her three boys. Three preachers! Mom says now, "The Lord answered my second prayer with my first prayer."

The question I hear from most of my peers nowadays is not, "What's wrong with your mom?" For the most part, people ask, "What's right with your mom?" Same answer: "She prays." That's the way she lived and still lives. Mom had, and still has, the mind of her Life Savior—a lifesaver mentality. She stayed and still stays in a right relationship with Him. She wants God's kingdom to come and His will to "be done on earth as it is in heaven" (Matt. 6:10). For Mom and her three preacher boys, relationships still rule.

REALISTIC EXPECTATION No. 4
BE HOLY SPIRIT RELIANT

Sixteen sweet words are at the end of 1 John 4:4: "The One who is in you is greater than the one who is in the world." When it comes to effective leadership, let us not forget that leadership is an inside joy before it ever becomes an outside job. In the case of Christian leadership, the Powerful Person within us, the Spirit of the Living Lord, must always be our greatest confidence.

I love the command of God in the opening words of Ps. 46:10: "Be still, and know that I am God." Before we attempt any style of leadership, let us first make sure we are living the Lordship lifestyle. Saturating in the presence of the Lord, being still before Him, is always the best way to remember that He is the Big Leader and we are the little leaders.

KING OF KINGS

A few years ago, I visited a castle in Europe. As the tour guide talked in the throne room, I was distracted by the inspiring painting on the dome ceiling above the throne. Inquisitive I asked, "What's up with the painting of Jesus returning in the clouds?" The reply enriched my life: "The king who lived in this castle had Jesus in all of His glory painted above the throne so he would not forget that he was the little king serving under the King of Kings."

It's true. As leaders we must never forget that we are serving under authority. We are not independent, but reliant. Jesus departed earth ascending into heaven, but the Spirit of our Living Lord remains to reign on the thrones of our hearts. I call it the Lordship lifestyle. Our confidence comes from knowing that the One who reigns within us is greater than any and all outside powers.

HALLELUJAH! WHAT'S IT TO YA?

In John 14, Jesus promised the Holy Spirit. We need the Holy Spirit, leaders. Have you read the verses lately? Hear again the words of promise. Take time to be still, to saturate and to celebrate in these wonderful words spoken by our Lord, verses 15 through 26:

> If you love me, obey my commandments. And I will ask the Father, and he will give you another Advocate, who will never leave you. He

is the Holy Spirit, who leads into all truth. The world cannot receive him, because it isn't looking for him and doesn't recognize him. But you know him, because he lives with you now and later will be in you. No, I will not abandon you as orphans—I will come to you. Soon the world will no longer see me, but you will see me. Since I live, you also will live. When I am raised to life again, you will know that I am in my Father, and you are in me, and I am in you. Those who accept my commandments and obey them are the ones who love me. And because they love me, my Father will love them. And I will love them and reveal myself to each one of them. Judas (not Judas Iscariot, but the other disciple with that name) said to him, "Lord, why are you going to reveal yourself only to us and not to the world at large?" Jesus replied, "All who love me will do what I say. My Father will love them, and we will come and make our home with each of them. Anyone who doesn't love me will not obey me. And remember, my words are not my own. What I am telling you is from the Father who sent me. I am telling you these things now while I am still with you. But when the Father sends the Advocate as my representative—that is, the Holy Spirit—he will teach you everything and will remind you of everything I have told you.

I don't know about you, but if I am going to lead, I want to be led by the Spirit of my Living Lord. Recently, I adopted a new theme in my life as a leader: *I don't always have to be right, just righteous.* In other words, "I don't have to know everything about everything all the time. I just need to be in a nonstop, up-to-date, right relationship with my God." The Spirit of my Living Lord reigning within me makes this a reality.

I don't have to be absolutely perfect. I just have to claim and cling to the awesome promise—the blessed Holy Spirit. Yes, because Jesus promised His Holy Spirit, I choose to claim His promise. Beyond good leadership principles, I place my confidence in the great leadership Person—the precious, promised Holy Spirit. Colossians 1:27 contains the greatest secret of confidence a leader could ever cling to: "And this is the secret: Christ lives in you" (NLT). Yes, because leadership is an inside joy, I can say to all outside influences, "Hallelujah! What's it to ya?"

HOLY SPIRIT OR HUMAN EFFORT

In Acts 1:8, Jesus offers us His heavenly power for earthly leadership. "But you will receive power when the Holy Spirit comes upon you. And you will be my witnesses, telling people about me everywhere—in Jerusalem, throughout Judea, in Samaria, and to the ends of the earth" (NLT). I choose to lead by being Holy Spirit reliant rather than depending on human effort. Likewise, I need leaders alongside me who rely on the Spirit of the Living Lord reigning inside them. It's a realistic leadership expectation.

The Book of Acts is simply the first volume of a continuing story. Acts records some of the things that the Holy Spirit empowered the believers of the first century to accomplish. The story is still unfolding through our leadership today. I believe that one day in heaven we will read from the Book of Acts, Volume 21 (for the twenty-first century). We will delightfully discover that our names along with the many mighty things performed through our lives by the Holy Spirit have also been recorded for eternity.

The Book of Acts literally tells us that because the Early Church leaders relied so totally on the Holy Spirit, they turned their world upside down. It's true. They were charged with changing the whole world. What made them so powerful? They were one in the Spirit. They were one in the Lord. Yes, the Holy Spirit gave them an inside unity that could not be conquered by outside forces. These great leaders of old surrendered their weak human efforts to God and received in return the wonder-working Holy Spirit. What really happened? These Holy Spirit reliant radicals did much more than make a difference in their world. They made their world different. Radically different!

As leaders, we find in Acts electrifying examples of effective leadership. Will we live from surrendered hearts too? Will we let go of our own weaknesses and live God-ordered, Jesus-led, and Spirit-filled lives? If we will, our leadership will make our world different.

THE REAL LORD'S PRAYER

"Our Father in heaven, hallowed be your name" (Matt. 6:9). In my opinion, what we refer to as the Lord's Prayer should really be called the Disciple's Prayer because it is the prayer that Jesus taught His disciples to pray. Now, make no mistake about it, I love the prayer. I pray it all the time. However, I find the *real* Lord's Prayer in John 17, because it's the prayer that the Lord prayed. I've often said that if I could only have one chapter from the Bible, I would choose John 17. Why? It is the personal prayer of my personal Lord. I believe that Jesus prayed the prayer in the presence of His disciples as they crossed the Kidron Valley, east of Jerusalem, on the way to Gethsemane on the night of His betrayal.

What is the main theme of the prayer Jesus prayed in John 17? What does Jesus ask the Father to give to His fully devoted followers? Jesus wants us to have *Oneness*. The power of unity is what the Lord most desperately desires for those who will be known as His disciples. Indeed, I believe the heart of the prayer is discovered in John 17:21: "I pray that they will all be one, just as you and I are one—as you are in me, Father, and I am in you. And may they be in us so that the world will believe you sent me" (NLT).

Every leader should spend saturation time in John 17. What better way to lead for the Lord than to know the desires of His heart. The prayer teaches us many things about our Leader, Jesus. For example, as I saturate in the real Lord's Prayer, I know for sure that *unity is the prayer of Jesus and division is the snare of Satan.* Just knowing that makes us more effective leaders because it also makes us more reliant on the Holy Spirit.

MY LEADERSHIP PRAYER FROM A SURRENDERED HEART

We know the Disciple's Prayer and the Lord's Prayer, but do you have a prayer? I challenge you to begin immediately praying and recording what might be known as your leadership prayer. Then keep editing, rewriting, and praying it all the days of your life. I have such a prayer that I started several years ago, and I'm still rewriting it. I call it my leadership prayer from a surrendered heart. As a leader, I know how very dependent I am upon divine power. Without the Holy Spirit in my life, I would not want to be known in any capacity as a leader. I hope that my very personal prayer journey proves the point that I am Holy Spirit reliant. Isn't it a realistic leadership

expectation to expect those who partner with me
to be Holy Spirit reliant too? I certainly think so.

Here's "My Leadership Prayer from a Surrendered Heart." I invite you to pray it with
me until you begin to compose your own:

Dearest Abba Father,

Please free me from all fear for this day . . .

from all anxiety about tomorrow . . .

from all bitterness toward another . . .

from all cowardice in the face of danger . . .

from all laziness in the necessity of work . . .

from all failure before opportunity . . .

from all weakness when Your power is so available.

Please free me, Lord, in You.

Please fill me with love that knows no limit . . .

with hope that knows no defeat . . .

with sympathy that embraces the hurting . . .

with courage that cannot be intimidated . . .

with strength adequate for life's challenges . . .

*with loyalty that proves my devo-
tion to You and to others . . .*

with release to soar on the wings of eagles . . .

with wisdom to match life's complexities . . .

with peace that silences me in every storm . . .

with faith that sees and glows in the dark.

Please fill me, Lord, with You.

Lord, I surrender myself to You completely . . .

and I gladly say YES to Your per-
fect will and Your divine way.
My delights, my desires find fulfill-
ment in Your holy presence.
Thank You for the gift of Your precious, loving Son . . .
and Your blessed Holy Spirit . . .
Today, I rededicate my best, my
all, my life, to Your glory.
In my life, Lord, be glorified today. In Your
Church, Lord, be glorified, I pray.
I plead Your blood and whisper Your name.
You are the One called Wonder-
ful—Jesus, my Life Savior!
Because of Your limitless love, O Lord,
I'm humbled, grateful, and . . . speech-
less. Amen, Amen, and Amen.

REALISTIC EXPECTATION No. 3
BE PRO-JESUS AND ANTI-SIN

At times, I hear people say, "Well, I'm no saint." That
kind of language falling from the lips of fully devoted
followers of Jesus confuses me. In fact, it infuri-
ates me. I'm sure that such a declaration is probably
meant to be a humble confession, but I truly believe it
is human arrogance mixed with ignorance. If I have
learned anything about being a Christian, it is this:
What might seem to be humility to us often is arrogance to God, and what might seem to be arrogance
to us is in actuality humility to God. To say, "Well, I'm
no saint," is to make Christianity mainly about our
human performance instead of about the holy presence of our Lord in our lives. Is it a stretch to say that
those who have Jesus reigning in their lives are, in
fact, *saints*? The songwriter hit the nail on the head
when he penned these words, "Oh I long to be in that
number / when the *saints* go marching *in*" (emphasis

93

added). The song does not declare, "Oh, I long to be in that number / when the *hain'ts** go marching *past*."

Here's my point: If Jesus came to do any one thing, it was to transform sinners into saints. At its most basic definition, that's what I mean when I say that I require those who serve in leadership alongside me to be *pro-Jesus and anti-sin*.

EXCLUSIVELY HIS

The best definition I've ever heard for "saint" requires only two words: "Exclusively His!" To be in love with Jesus is to be *exclusively His*. It's not a duty thing. It's a devotion thing. It baffles me when people who claim to love the Lord say they cannot be expected to totally turn their backs on sin and belong totally to Him. How such an attitude must break the heart of God. We expect more from a person-to-person relationship than we expect in our person-to-God relationship. How sad is that? How wrong is that? It's beyond sad and wrong. It's sick and warped.

Suppose when my wife and I were married, shortly after speaking my vows to my new bride, I looked at her and said, "Honey, I really do love you, but for the honeymoon I've invited my old girlfriend to join us. Oh, I will be yours 99.9 percent of the

---

*"Hain't" is Southern fisherman's slang for someone who isn't genuine. Here the word can also refer to those who "hain't" (aren't) going to make it into heaven.

time, but I will be having a short walk each day in the park with her." *No way* is right. We'd never allow such an arrangement in our husband-to-wife relationship, yet we say to Jesus, "I want to belong to You; however, my old pal, sin, is still going to be a small part of my life." *No way* is right again.

When we turn to Jesus, He expects us to turn our backs on sin. After all, He has already warned us that He is indeed a jealous God. Guess what? My wife is a jealous wife, too, and I'm glad she is. In the marriage relationship, she expects me to be *exclusively hers.* Likewise, in the spiritual relationship, my Lord expects me to be *exclusively His.* I call it pro-Jesus and anti-sin. The old saying is very true: "Jesus will either be Lord of all, or Lord not at all." It sounds like a realistic expectation to me. How about you? Why would we ever expect more in the marriage relationship than we expect in our relationships with the Master?

NO MORE OLD FLAMES

Let me accent the fidelity principle with a story I once heard. A mother was attending a wedding with her college son. During the ceremony the bride and groom lit the traditional unity candle and then extinguished their own candles. The mother leaned over to her son and whispered, "What do you suppose the true meaning of lighting a big candle and blowing out the little candles really means?" His spontaneous reply was classic: "That's simple, Mom. No more old flames."[1]

Yes, simple, yet profound. Fully devoted followers of Jesus are fiery with passion for their Lord to the point of extinguishing all other competing lights. It's not that we cannot sin. It's just that we are so singularly focused on our Savior that sin loses its appeal to us, as does anything else next to our devotion to Him. My twenty-seven-year-old friend, Philip Zimmermann, shared an awesome insight with me along these lines. Citing the writer of Hebrews, and the idea of "throw[ing] off everything that hinders and the sin that so easily entangles" (12:1), Philip said, "I want my life to be so focused on Jesus that I not only turn my back on sin—the bad—but also on every other weight that hinders, even the good weights." That's it, my friends. To be pro-Jesus and anti-sin is to say and to pray, "My God, no more new games, no more old flames. I want to burn for You alone here on earth and throughout eternity. I want to give my best for Your glory." Don't focus on sin. Focus on Him. What would you call a person like that? A saint! Someone who is exclusively His!

POWER STRUGGLE

I have trouble with a theology that believes sin is more powerful than God. While other churches are cursing the darkness, I want to lead our local body of believers in such a way that we declare, "So, the world is dark? What's the big deal? We have the candles!" In the power struggle between light and darkness, shadows don't have a fighting chance against our God's beam. God's beam has a name—Jesus, and we need to let Him shine through us. As a child, many of us cut our spiritual teeth on a tune with a similar message: "This little light of mine, / I'm gonna let it shine."

What do you suppose would happen in the spiritual power struggle we're in if all of us would just bring our little lights together and let them shine? Darkness would be dispelled. Sin would cave in. That's exactly what would happen. Do you suppose that if we could just get our little Jesus lights lifted up in this dark world, those lost in darkness would run to the Light of the World? Friends, if we are truly pro-Jesus and anti-sin, we are the people with the Power. As we allow Jesus to live His life through us, to shine His light through us, such powerful, personal worship increases His wonderful wattage and the whole world can go from the shadows of human sin to the highlights of His holiness. Darkness trembles when we as saints get the candles out. Darkness runs when we as saints strike the matches against the Master. Darkness hides when we lift our little lights toward the heavenly realms. If we will turn the lights out on sin, the Light of the World will turn on and begin to burn brightly.

Wonder if it's really true? Would something wonderful really happen in our world if those of us who claim to belong to God really turned from sin and turned to Him? Read these words from the Old Testament book of 2 Chron. 7:14 and decide for yourself: "If my people, who are called by my name, will humble themselves and pray and seek my face and turn from their wicked ways, then will I hear from heaven and will forgive their sin and heal their land."

Pretty plain, isn't it? Sounds as if God has left the healing of our lands in the palm of our hands. He does not say, "If *the wicked* will become *my people,* healing will happen." He does say, "If *my people* will turn from *their wicked ways,* healing will happen."

I need those on my leadership team who believe the church is called to repent from within, not rebuke the rebellious ones all around us. The power struggle is primarily an inside-the-church diagnosis, not an outside-the-church discussion. We will not be defeated by outer darkness if we get the inner lights shining where the shadows are falling. The shadows are closer to the church than we realize.

A BEACON OF PERFECT LOVE AND PREVAILING HOPE

Without doubt, being the son of a fisherman makes me understand more clearly what being a fisherman for the Son is about. I was raised with great reverence for coastal lighthouses. For as many generations back that our family can recall, our fathers and grandfathers have been seamen. Long before electronic technology and The Weather Channel came to be, my forefathers had to place their confidence in sea experience and lighthouses. Yes, fishermen surely understand the validity of any gospel song that depicts Jesus as the Lighthouse. Such songs are symbolic of Jesus being our Beacon of Hope and the Guide of our souls. In the same way that land beacons have guided and continue to guide lost sailors into safe harbors, our loving Lord lights our way.

As He did with Peter in John 21, the Lord also called me from the shoreside to the sheep country. I was born and raised on a tiny island near the Atlantic Ocean. I pastor in a farming community in the heart of the Shenandoah Valley. Still, when it was time to define our focus, I had to cast a vision that I understood. As a result, our church is a beacon of perfect love and prevailing hope in the Shenandoah Valley and beyond. That's our identity statement. It might seem strange to some. How could lifesaving language and seaside slogans ever be effective hundreds of miles from the ocean? Believe it or not, it works wondrously.

I know that the one word in our identity statement that serves as a magnet on the souls of the lost is the word "hope." I once had a very educated, white-collar, prebeliever friend tell me the only thing we as a church could offer him that he couldn't find better somewhere else was *hope*. Hope means different things to different people, but there is no greater message of hope for souls bound by sin than to hear us say, "There really is a Savior, a Deliverer, who loves us so much that He came from heaven to earth. He came to save the sinner from sins, to bring forgiveness for the sinful acts that lead to death, and to deliver us from sinful attitudes that deliver only devastation. Jesus came to give His life for sin's destruction so sin couldn't destroy our lives for eternity. Yes, there is hope in knowing that Christ became sin for us on the Cross so we could become His saints in this world."

There is no greater hope than to be freed from what's killing us, and Jesus came to do this—to be our hope. As His beacons, our lives must send out this two-part, glorious gleam across the angry waves of life: Our God's love never fails and His hope always prevails. Even for you. Especially for you!

The message our Savior wants us to hear and to share is indeed good news: Love won! Hope too! It's not about principles, but a Person. Let us never forget that God's love and hope have a name—Jesus. Neither rebellion nor religion can offer true love or real hope to the seemingly loveless and hopeless, but a relationship with Jesus can, will, and does.

When it comes to light, Jesus is the Real Thing. We're entrusted with the awesome privilege of being mirrors that reflect His love and hope to the world. Yes, we are called to be the lighthouses. He is the Light!

For a coastal boy, few things are sadder than a lighthouse without light. I once visited the two lighthouses at Cape Henry located on the eastern seaboard near Virginia Beach, Virginia. The older of the two lighthouses is actually the oldest light-house in the United Sates. Our first president, George Washington, commissioned it. I paid a few dollars to climb the old structure of hope. As I panted breath-lessly up the final steps toward the light tower, my heart was broken. Why? There was no light at the top. Standing there, I couldn't help but think about the church. How often is the church only a structure lacking substance? A lighthouse without a light is not a lighthouse; it is only a house. A lighthouse without a light may have a fine reputation for being a beacon of hope, a friend of sailors, but in reality it is only a dungeon of darkness, not at all a friend of sinners.

As a church leader, I shudder when I consider several final New Testament words from the mouth of the Glorified Christ. He is addressing the churches in the Book of Revelation. The first words that shake me up, in Rev. 2:4-5, are spoken to the church at Ephesus. The other shivering words, in Rev. 3:1-2, are spoken to the church at Sardis. Allow me to give the words together. Remember this is Jesus talking:

> I have this complaint against you. You don't love me or each other as you did at first! Look how far you have fallen! Turn back to me and do the works you did at first. If you don't repent, I will come and remove your lampstand from its place among the churches. . . . I know all the things you do, and that you have a reputation for being alive—but you are dead. Wake up! Strengthen what little remains, for even what is left is almost dead. I find that your actions do not meet the requirements of my God.

When I read these words that the One who is the Head of the Body, the Christ, spoke to the ones who are His Body, the Church, I do indeed grow fainthearted. What I hear Jesus saying is very plain: "As you love Me and each other, so My light either shines or does not shine to the world. In fact, the level of your love for Me and each other defines how much love and hope you really offer the world." Simply said, "The level of our love determines the quality of the fuel that shines the light of hope from our lighthouses." Jesus warned His church at Ephesus and warns His church everywhere else. He clearly says, "Church, if you do not repent, if you do not return to your first love, I will come and remove my light from your lighthouse. It will be the night the lights go out in Ephesus and everywhere else."

The church at Sardis was in a similar situation. They had a mere reputation for being alive, but they were, in fact, dead. Sixteen words come to mind and I earnestly pray them for the church I pastor: "Dearest Lord, if that is true of us, please, now forgive it and later forbid it." I once heard an old-time evangelist say, "A funeral director can make a corpse look better than a living person, but it's still dead." I know it's possible for a church leader, full of human charisma but lacking in holy character, to make a church appear alive when in fact it is dead. How can we prevent such a scary scenario? First and foremost, as individual leaders, we must not only have a reputation for being pro-Jesus and anti-sin but also live it and shine it! If we will be saints privately, then the Lord will entrust us to operate lighthouses publicly.

Let us never compromise as His beacons of perfect love and prevailing hope by substituting watered-down fuels. Our Master's holy, high-octane mixture is proven by two words: *love* and *hope*.

REALISTIC EXPECTATION No. 2
BE AN INTERCESSOR FOR GOD

Ezekiel 22:30 contains fourteen words that move
me toward true intercession for God: "I searched
for someone to stand in the gap . . . but I found no
one" (NLT). How sad is that? Hallelujah, we still have
Isa. 6:8: "Then I heard the Lord asking, 'Whom
should I send as a messenger to this people? Who
will go for us?' I said, 'Here I am. Send me'" (NLT).

I VOLUNTEERED TO GOD

Isaiah 6:8 helped me crystallize my call to
ministry and church leadership. I was already in
my first year as Vision Pastor at the First Church
of the Nazarene in Harrisonburg, Virginia. Earlier in Bible college I had heard other ministry
students talk about how God called them to min-

105

istry. I could not, with integrity, make that same declaration. Finally, during that first year in the pastorate, while reading from Oswald Chambers's classic devotional *My Utmost for His Highest,* I can only say that the witness of the Spirit came.

I can best describe my call this way: "I heard my Triune God saying, 'We're looking for someone to go for Us,' and, like Brother Isaiah, I volunteered to go for my Triune God." I was not drafted to serve the Lord out of duty. I surrendered and said out of devotion, "If You can use me, Lord, I'm exclusively Yours. If You're looking for someone to stand in the gap for You, here I am. Send me." Read Brother Chambers's January 14 selection based on Isa. 6:8 and you will understand what I'm saying.

An intercessor for God is just that—one who surrenders and says, "I'll gladly stand in the gap for You, my God. I volunteer to You, my God. You give the orders; I'll take the orders. I want to know You above everyone else. I want to go for You anywhere and everywhere You say to go." Being an intercessor for God means I will say what He says to say and I will pray what He says to pray. God asks, "Who will?" I answer, "I will!" Likewise, I hold this realistic leadership expectation up to those who serve with me on our local church leadership team. Go to God. Go for God. Gladly!

CHOOSE INTIMACY OR IDOLATRY

A few years ago, I came before the Lord with a heavy heart. I confessed to God that I was not satisfied with my personal prayer life. I especially felt like a failure in intercessory prayer. As I sought the Lord with all of my heart concerning this issue, He began to answer me through His Word. Specifically, He spoke to me from what's referred to as the Great Commandments. With my ears wide open, I listened to Luke 10:27: "'You must love the Lord your God with all your heart, all your soul, all your strength, and all your mind.' And, 'Love your neighbor as yourself'" (NLT).

What was the Lord whispering to my wondering heart? He was whispering that I had a *wandering* heart. From His Word, He spoke to my attentive soul: "Kerry, you are failing at intercessory prayer because you are on the verge of choosing idolatry over intimacy." Yes, I was troubled to say the least. I continued to consider Luke 10:27 for understanding and correction. "Kerry, you are getting too close to moving the second great commandment above the first great commandment in your praying. When you pray, you often place what people want from Me over what I will for them. You are to represent Your God above your people. People are too often concerned about Me making them happy, but I am always more concerned about making people holy."

As a dear man of God in my life, Dr. Neil Wiseman, says, "I had an 'Aha!' moment." Immediately, I repented and ever since that heart-wrenching encounter with my God, I have continued to compassionately emphasize the requests of people to God, but I have first and foremost passionately empathized with God. I choose intimacy with Him, not idolatry with them. *What He wills* is much more important that *what we want.*

PRAY NOW!

I wish I could remember who taught me on-the-spot praying. It has been perhaps the most valuable form of ministering God to people that I practice. On any given day, people approach Christian leaders saying, "Would you pray for me? Would you pray for my child? Would you pray for my family?" And the list goes on. I once heard John Maxwell say that a man approached him in the foyer of the church and asked that his pastor would pray for him in the areas of tithing. John said he immediately placed his hand on his brother, closed his eyes, and lifted his voice in public prayer. As I recall, the very vocal, public prayer went something like this: "Lord, my brother is robbing You of Your tithe. Help him quickly to repent from thievery and begin returning to You what's already Yours. Amen." It's a funny example. However, John was onto something holy as well as humorous. First of all, John prayed on-the-spot with the parishioner. Second, he did not merely cuddle the would-be giver at the expense of not representing God's will for His people to be obedient and generous in the stewardship of tithes and offerings.

We have all read Mal. 3. Some leaders try to explain it away and may often delay in praying God's will for those they have been entrusted to represent God to. Others just choose to represent the Lord and immediately pray that God's will would begin to happen in the hearts of His people. John Maxwell's story is just one humorous and holy example of a good prayer to *pray in the here and now*. Thanks, John. You da man! God's man!

As a pastor, I carry a bottle of anointing oil in my pocket at all times. It's a James 5 thing. I never know when someone will come to me in the church foyer, in the department store, or at the gas pump and say, "Pastor, will you pray for me. I need the Lord's touch in my life." I don't delay such divine appointments. I pray immediately and intimately wherever I might encounter such requests. I think it's one of the easiest ways to allow Jesus to minister through us. When I was ordained, the general superintendent told me, "Be ready in season and out of season." When I choose to pray in the here and now, I sense more than ever that I am right in line and on time with my joyful job description as a minister of Good News. Nearly every time I surprise a person in need, by offering for them on-the-spot praying, tears begin to flow before I say, "Amen." Could it be that these spontaneously sown tears will bring a harvest of joy? I would say so. If the question is, "Pray how?" The answer is, "Pray now!"

Those who join me in leadership are expected to pray without delay. Not only does it minister God's will to the hurting, but it also causes us to live in up-to-date, intimate relationships with the Lord at all times. Such on-the-spot praying is an opportunity to offer the compassion of Christ to others, but even more essentially, on-the-spot readiness is a call for us as church leaders to live our lives transparently and passionately with un-questionable intimacy before a healing, holy God. Let us not neglect any of the verses in James 5. The one needing the prayer may need compassion and healing, but the one offering the prayer must not live short of confession and holiness either.

PRAY WITH AND FOR ONE ANOTHER

Want to have a surprising and inspiring Bible drill? Investigate the powerful stories of people praying together. Prayer closets are powerful, but prayer teams are pretty potent too. Two examples of what happens when believers join together in

prayer are found in two New Testament accounts:
(1) the Day of Pentecost and (2) the freeing of the
apostle Peter from prison. The Book of Acts accents
the holy habit of praying with and for one another.

Too often I fear that prayer is more of a lecture
in our churches than it is a laboratory. The last thing
most believers need is another group talk on prayer.
What we desperately need is a group walk where we
actually pray together. Several times a year we turn
our weekly worship services into prayer laboratories.
We call the services Gethsemane Gatherings. The idea
is to somehow give Jesus back that hour of prayer
that the disciples slept through on the night He was
betrayed. Throughout each of our Gethsemane Gatherings, we simply pray together. Often people kneel
continuously as the Lord leads. Prayer songs are
sung. Communion elements are distributed. Anointing is offered for those who need a healing touch.
Without exception, once the services have ended,
many worshipers come to me and say, "Pastor, these
prayer laboratories are life-changing." We should not
be surprised. Corporate praying is modeled throughout God's Word as wonder-working and wonderful.

THE PASTOR'S PRAYER PATROL

Around 6 A.M. each Tuesday, vehicles pull onto
our church parking lot as men gather to pray with
and for their pastor. The official name of our com-

ing together is the Pastor's Prayer Patrol. I often refer to it as the Dawn Patrol. It is without doubt my favorite event on our entire church calendar. It all began twelve, maybe fourteen, years ago with two or three men joining me in my church office to seek the Lord together. Now we have moved into one of the largest rooms in our building for this early morning God-seeking session. If there's any secret to what the Lord has done, is doing, and still wants to do in the life of our local church body, this Tuesday morning men's gathering might be it.

Once, I was telling another pastor about the Pastor's Prayer Patrol. He said, "The Pastor's Prayer Patrol sounds somewhat arrogant to me." His emphasis was on "the Pastor's" Prayer Patrol. I gently but firmly replied, "What really seems like arrogance to me is a pastor who won't admit that he needs a prayer patrol. I call it 'the Pastor's Prayer Patrol' mostly as a public confession that I need God-seekers on my side." The point was well received.

I do, indeed, need a prayer team as a team leader. I personally need to be continuously in the throne room of the great God who joins us when we pray together. He promised if we would come together in His name, He would show up. Doesn't God also show up with us in our individual prayer times? Sure, He does. In fact, not only do the men show up on Tuesday mornings at the church for corporate prayer, but they also choose one day of the week to pray separately for me. Still, when we do come together to pray, evidently something else even more wonderful happens in our lives. Could it be that our coming together to pray actually allows God to move beyond *showing up in our lives* to also *showing off in our lives*?

HEAD UP! KNEES DOWN!

My fisherman dad has a favorite saying that he lives by. He also encourages others to live by it: "If you're gonna hang your head, hang it up so you can see the face of God." Over the years, I have taken my dad's words as my own and added an extra idea as well: "Keep your head up and your knees down!" I love the Old Testament leader Nehemiah. One thing about his life I want to imitate. He was a leader from the knees up. It was less of a physical posture and more of a heart hunger. Nehemiah wanted to be a servant in the hands of his God. Persistent praying proved the passionate position of his heart.

A person who prays continuously is a person surrendered to be a servant in the hands of God. Praying says, "Spirit of the Living God, live Your will through my life." That's what I really mean by "heads up and knees down." It's a word picture of a surrendered heart. Most people know Rom. 8:28 by heart, but verses 26-27 speak to the heart of praying: "And the Holy Spirit helps us in our weakness. For example, we don't know what God wants us to pray for. But the Holy Spirit prays for us with groanings that cannot be expressed in words. And the Father who knows all hearts knows what the Spirit is saying, for the Spirit pleads for us believers in harmony with God's own will" (NLT).

Wow! What does God desire? He desires surrendered hearts filled with His own Holy Spirit that He can flow through in order to accomplish His own perfect will. So what is prayer all about? Praying is an invitation for me to be an intercessor for God. For me, prayer is all about intimacy with the Almighty, yes, indescribable and undeniable closeness with Christ. As the Spirit of my Living God possesses me, as He flows through me and prays through me, I know deep within me that this relationship is really what prayer is all about.

REALISTIC EXPECTATION №. 1
BREATHE PROACTIVE LOYALTY

She was three years old. It was our daddy-and-daughter date day. After a ride on the paddle wheel ferryboat, we took a walk on the beach where we drew words in the sand. In my mind's eye, I can still see our sand-scribbled message: "Daddy loves Allison and Allison loves Daddy." A giant-sized heart surrounded our simple but profound artwork.

After our fun in the sun, we stopped for her first visit to a Chinese restaurant. Sitting in the dimly lit atmosphere, my darling daughter sat on her knees, leaned over the candlelight, and whispered, "Daddy, why is it so dark in here?" I whispered back in a sacred voice, "This is a romantic atmosphere, Precious. It's a special place where people who really love each other come to eat." With a gleam in her eye for the only man in her life, her daddy, little, precious Allison gave me a wonder-filled expression followed by a sacred whisper: "We really love each other, Daddy!" That was the day I taught my daughter how to eat with chopsticks and the day my daughter taught me she could steal her daddy's heart.

LOYALTY IS LOVE IN MOTION

Those who lead alongside me must prove their claims of love by practicing loyalty. Loyalty is love in motion. Loyalists are never passive bystanders but are always passionate defenders of love, seeking unity for the glory of God, for the good of their families, and for the growth of their leadership teams.

As I declared earlier, I am a lifelong learner. I seek to always have a green-apple attitude, always growing and never quite totally ripe, because once I'm ripe, I realize that rotting is the only stage left. And as I also said, one of my most recent lessons in the lifelong school of learning is that "I don't always have to be right, but I always have to be righteous." By this I mean, I don't always have to have the last word, but I always have to prove my love through my loyalty. I will not always be right, but I must always seek to be in right relationship with my Lord, my family, my partners in leadership, and beyond. Loving God and loving people is my calling. For me, love and loyalty combine to purify the heartbeat of life—relationships.

THREEFOLD LOYALTY

The No. 1 realistic expectation that I present to those who will partner alongside me is proactive loyalty. Proactive loyalty is not a self-preserving ego trip to protect me as the lead pastor. No, proactive loyalty is much more than that. Proactive loyalty is an essential shield for guarding God-given relationships across the board. Loyalty as I see it is threefold in its description: (1) don't betray our God, (2) don't betray your family, and (3) don't betray your pastor.

When I consider the original disciples of Jesus, my mind sees two extremes: John the Beloved and Judas the Betrayer. Both were given the choice about being proactively loyal to our Lord. You know how the personal stories ended. Judas the Betrayer committed suicide, and believe it or not, in some regions of the world certain Christians doubt whether John the Beloved ever died. Here's my point: as disciples who desire to lead alongside the Lord, we, like the first followers of Christ, still have a choice to make. Will we be proactive loyalists or will we be passive betrayers? Will we be loyal to God, loyal to our families, and loyal to our leaders? If we cannot be loving and loyal to one another as leaders, chances are we will fail our families and God in love and loyalty as well.

LOYALTY IS LOUD

Maybe you're wondering exactly what I mean by *proactive loyalty*. Here's exactly what I mean. Proactive loyalty is loud. Betrayal is silent. Proactive loyalists speak out. Betrayers blend in. Loyalists seek to properly defend their leaders. Betrayers seek to privately save themselves. For example, as leader partners, we need to think more than twice before engaging in what is often referred to as "behind-the-back, constructive criticism of a person's competence." Often such rationale is really "between-the-shoulder-blades, destructive assassination of a person's character."

Here is an example of what loyalty is not. When I leave the pulpit in the hands of another pastor while I'm on vacation, the loyalty test begins when the parishioners comment on sermons preached in my absence. Now those on our leadership team are all great communicators, so I'm always confident that I am leaving the pulpit in very capable hands. But suppose one of the hearers of the most recent sermon says to one of my partner pastors: "That was one great sermon. I wish you preached every Sunday?" Hold your breath, my friends, because my leadership partner is about to be graded? Will he or she pass or fail? Will he or she breathe loyalty, or will he or she breathe betrayal? Will the lead preacher be defended, or will the preacher-of-the-day elevate his or her own personal résumé? Being silent will indicate a subtle but sure lack of proactive loyalty.

Friends, it's true. Loyalty is loud. Betrayal is silent. A true lover of the lead preacher will speak the truth in love. One of two comments should be the response to such an ego-building comment: (1) "Now, we both know who the lead preacher is here and it is not me. I'm just blessed to partner alongside Pastor Kerry" or (2) "I will not receive a compliment at the expense of my lead preacher and friend, Pastor Kerry." That's pretty blunt, pastor? Blunt is right and being blunt is many times the proper way to prove proactive loyalty.

Nothing dispels a passive betrayer better than a proactive loyalist who always devotedly and deliberately speaks the *truth in love*. Love is loud. Love is spoken. When it comes to realistic expectations, all I really expect from my leadership partners is the same declaration of love that my darling daughter spoke to me in the Chinese restaurant: "We really love each other."

ONE STEP HIGHER

Let's take this loyalty conversation one step higher. If you feel you cannot be proactively loyal to your leader, change teams—and the sooner the better. If you cannot trust the team you are on, it is not too late to seek a new locker room. Understand that

I do not expect blind trust or flimsy faith in a leader you cannot follow. That would only serve to breed an integrity virus. Don't substitute lying for loyalty. However, if you wear the colors of your pastor-coach, then guard your pastor-coach's back and defend those you share the locker room and the field with.

Some people have trouble being under authority. It is a scary thing to me. I believe the Bible clearly communicates that a person who cannot be trusted under authority can never be trusted over authority. Even Jesus made His mission clear. He came to do His Father's will. Talk about proactive loyalty. He came to speak His Father's words. What an example for us to imitate! Actually, that is the real way we as leaders will live out true love and loyalty, by letting the Spirit of the Living God reign on the thrones of our lives.

LOYALTY IS A TWO-WAY STREET

If I expect those around me to breathe proactive loyalty, rest assured, it only means that I will inhale and exhale the same loving lifestyle for those who join me in ministry. One day I might be able to write a book and give actual names, but for now just take my word for it: I have properly defended those who partner with me in ministry in ways that only heaven will reveal. No, I do not defend immorality or godless living. That would only be blind loyalty.

However, those who are on our team in good faith know that I have their backs. On occasion I have even had to prove my loyalty for my partners in ministry to members of my own family. Each time so far, I have come away with new respect from my own family and new rejoicing in my own soul.

As Christ-centered leadership teams, we must choose to be families of faith, hope, and love. Good faith, real hope, and true love are reinforced best by proactive loyalty. In fact, I honestly believe that proactive loyalty must be the air that we continuously breathe.

To breathe proactive loyalty for our God, our families, and our leadership teams is to attract the world exactly the way our Lord said we would. What did Jesus say? "Your love for one another will prove that you are my disciples" (NLT). Two-way love and loyalty is the fuel that keeps our Christ beacons of love and hope burning brightly to a lost and seemingly loveless world. When the world sees undeniable unity in our ranks as the church, hope begins to shine in invaluable ways.

ONE FINAL STORY

I wrote this whole book to tell you one final story. It's true. Without this story, there would be no book. Without this story, I would know virtually nothing about real leadership. Whatever I

know about leadership, my fisherman dad taught
me under the big oak tree in our front yard when
I was just sixteen years old. But before I tell you
the story, let me give you a little background.

My life began in the midst of a paradox. I was
raised in one of the most relational but also perhaps
most religious places on the planet—Harkers Island,
North Carolina. In our church we had the best and
the worst of both worlds. We had a delicate balance
of love and legalism. At church, I could have given up
on God because of the confusing atmosphere coming
from all that was religious. At home, however, I could
not give up on God because of the clear atmosphere
coming from all that was relational. Perhaps the
greatest paradox of my early years was the fact that I
did not understand that a public religion designed by
humans and a private relationship with God are not
necessarily one in the same. The miracle is that in our
family my parents somehow struggled with both, but
in the end, the relational won out over the religious.

This victory of the relational over the religious
becomes especially clear in this story I'm about to
tell. It's about how my dad set the direction for the
rest of my life without even realizing it. As you read,
keep in mind what I stated at the beginning of this
book: "Everything really rises and falls on relationship. Even leadership. Especially leadership."

June 12, 1977, was a day I never thought would arrive. It was the day I turned sixteen, and I wanted my driver's license. Yes, I wanted a license more than anything in the world. Almost a full year earlier I had purchased a car to call my own. Working on my dad's shrimp boat during the summers and working at Best Supermarket during my high school years had allowed me to get my very own car—a 1976 Monte Carlo. It had a 400 block engine with a four-barrel carburetor. Four shiny wheels— complete with wide, white-letter tires—made this vehicle of my dreams virtually irresistible.

When the day finally came, I passed my driver's test on the first try and quickly raced home to drop off Mom, who had driven me to the testing station, so I could finally cruise solo around the roads of my native, eastern North Carolina homeland. For a teenage boy, life doesn't get any better than that.

Before I left the island to make my first trip to town, I asked Dad to come in the front yard. In somewhat of a hurry, I quickly asked, "What are the rules, Dad?" He gave me a blank stare as if to say, "I don't know what you're talking about, Son." So I repeated my plea: "Come on, Dad. Give me the rules. You know, give me the speech. What are your expectations?" Again, he just gave me a blank stare. So I continued what seemed to be a one-way, weird conversation. "Dad, I just got my driver's license. Soon

I will be leaving here in a car without you or Mom. Tell me, Dad, what are the rules? Give me the speech. What is my curfew? I need to hear your expectations."

At that moment, I remember tears welling up in my dad's eye sockets. Lovingly he looked through my eyes and deep into my soul. Then slowly he finally said, "Kerry, there are no rules. There is no speech. There is no curfew. Son, your mom and I have tried to raise you as best we could. You were our first of three boys, so we're sure we made many mistakes. Still, I think you know, Kerry, one thing is for sure; we've always loved you. When you leave here in your car all alone, you will be in control of your own life. We can only trust you. So there are no rules." Dad paused and then continued: "The only thing your mom and I ask of you is this: 'Please, Son, don't break our hearts.'"

With that, my dear dad turned and walked back into the house to be with Mom and left me standing all alone and weak-kneed beside my muscle car. On that day, I received both a license and a lesson—a legal license to drive and a life lesson on leadership. I wrote this whole book to tell you this one final story and to leave you with the words my dad left with me on my sixteenth birthday. Yes, under the old oak tree, I adopted one realistic leadership expectation for my life and for those who would dare to lead alongside me. I can frame it in one simple, yet profound statement: When relationships rule, there's little need for rules!

What should our one realistic leadership expectation be within the local church and beyond? All we should ask for can be communicated clearly in a threefold, sacred whisper: "Please don't break the heart of your God. Please don't break the hearts of your family members. Please don't break our hearts." Together, let's lead in a way that demonstrates we really love each other. Let's breathe proactive loyalty. That's really all we should expect.

NOTES

Chapter 4

1. Author's paraphrase from David McCasland, *Oswald Chambers: Abandoned to God: The Life Story of the Author of My Utmost for His Highest* (Grand Rapids: Discovery House, 1993), 177.

Chapter 7

1. John H. Sammis, "Trust and Obey," in *Sing to the Lord* (Kansas City: Lillenas Publishing Co., 1993), 437.

2. Judson W. Van DeVenter, "I Surrender All," in *Sing to the Lord*, 486 (emphasis added).

Chapter 8

1. Ray Lasalle, heard by author at a revival, Free Grace Wesleyan Church, Harkers Island, N.C., in the 1970s.

Chapter 11

1. Several versions of this story can be found on the Internet, but the author is unknown.